Wanda E. Brunstetter's

Amish Friends

One-Pan Wonders

Cookbook

Over 200 Recipes for Simplifying Mealtime

BARBOUR
PUBLISHING

© 2023 by Wanda E. Brunstetter

Print ISBN 978-1-63609-525-7

All scripture quotations are taken from the King James Version of the Bible.

Cover Top Photograph: Doyle Yoder, dypinc.com

Published by Barbour Publishing, Inc., 1810 Barbour Drive, Uhrichsville, OH 44683, www.barbourbooks.com

Our mission is to inspire the world with the life-changing message of the Bible.

 Member of the
Evangelical Christian
Publishers Association

Printed in China.

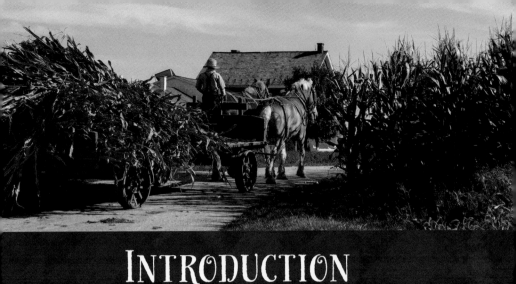

INTRODUCTION

We all seem to have busy lives these days, and often there isn't time to fix a big meal with several accompaniments. With my busy schedule, I appreciate meals that are quick and simple to make, yet healthy, stress-free, and with easy cleanup. When I am able to cook a one-pan meal, often no extra side dishes are necessary, so it makes meal prep even more enjoyable for me.

The *Amish Friends One-Pan Wonders Cookbook* includes recipes for supper, breakfast, desserts, salads, soups, and quick breads. Many of the recipes can be baked in the oven or cooked in a kettle or skillet on a stovetop with very little need to babysit the pan.

My husband and I have had the pleasure of eating meals and snacks in many of our Amish friends' homes. Several of the recipes they have shared with me were made in one pan. Making an effort to eat healthy and cook with low carbs and less sugar, I have enjoyed fixing many meals in one skillet on the stove, a baking dish for the oven, or using my slow cooker. These always include some form of protein and at least one healthy vegetable.

I hope you will enjoy the variety of delicious one-pan recipes in this cookbook that are served in Amish homes—either for family meals or at various community functions. The recipes include some of the best of the best from past Amish Friends cookbooks.

I wish to thank my editor, Rebecca Germany, for compiling this cookbook.

"Whether therefore ye eat, or drink, or whatsoever ye do,
do all to the glory of God" (1 Corinthians 10:31).

WANDA E. BRUNSTETTER

Contents

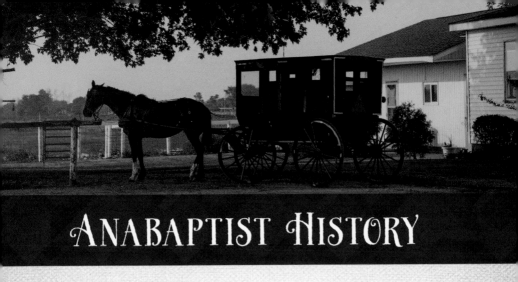

Anabaptist History

The Amish and Mennonites are direct descendants of the Anabaptists, a group that emerged from the Reformation in Switzerland in 1525 and developed separately in Holland a few years later. Most Anabaptists eventually became identified as Mennonites, after a prominent Dutch leader, Menno Simons. The word *Amish* comes from Jacob Ammann, an influential leader who in 1693 led a group that separated from the Mennonite churches. Driven by persecution from their homes in Switzerland and Germany, hundreds of Mennonites began to immigrate to North America, and in the 1700s the Amish sought homes in North America too. They were welcomed in Pennsylvania by William Penn and first settled there by the mid-nineteenth century.

As Amish communities continued to grow and seek more land, new Amish communities were started in other areas. Some moved to Ohio, Indiana, Iowa, and other parts of the country. Today there are Amish communities in many parts of the United States and Canada, and new ones continue to appear. The Amish population has grown to over three hundred thousand nationwide.

While all Amish adhere to the regulation of their *Ordnung* (church rules), many communities differ in practice, appearance, style of their homes, and types of buggies.

Both the Amish and Mennonites believe in the inerrant authority of the scriptures, and their willingness to stand apart from the rest of the world shows through their simple, plain way of living.

Everywhere Amish settle, their baked goods are sought after at farmers markets, flea markets, roadside stands, and bakeries, and their craftmanship in construction and woodworking is highly appreciated.

Special Request Breakfast Casserole

30 saltine crackers

6 eggs, beaten

6 slices bacon, cooked
and crumbled

2 cups milk

2 cups shredded cheddar cheese

¼ cup butter or
margarine, melted

Crumble crackers into 8x8-inch dish (double recipe to fit 9x13-inch pan). Combine remaining ingredients and pour over crackers. Cover and chill overnight. Remove from refrigerator 30 minutes before baking uncovered at 325 degrees for 45 minutes. Let stand 5 minutes before cutting and serving.

Mary Ellen Wengerd, Campbellsville, KY

Bacon and Egg Bake

6 slices bacon

1 medium onion, sliced

1 can cream of mushroom soup

½ cup milk

5 hard-boiled eggs, chopped

1 cup shredded cheddar cheese

Salt and pepper to taste

In skillet, fry bacon until crisp; drain fat. Use 2 tablespoons bacon fat to sauté onion. Stir in soup, milk, eggs, cheese, salt, and pepper. Pour into 6x10-inch dish. Top with crumbled bacon. Bake at 350 degrees for 20 minutes. Serve over toast or English muffins.

Elaine Nolt, Ephrata, PA

Overnight Breakfast Casserole

8 slices bread, cubed

¾ pound cheese, shredded

1½ pounds pork sausage or 1 quart canned sausage

4 eggs

2½ cups milk

1 tablespoon mustard

1 (10¾ ounce) can cream of mushroom or cream of chicken soup

¼ cup chicken broth

Place bread cubes in ungreased baking dish. Sprinkle with cheese. Set aside. In skillet, brown sausage over medium heat; drain fat. (If using canned sausage, skip the frying step.) Crumble sausage over cheese and bread. Beat eggs, milk, mustard, soup, and broth. Pour over sausage. Cover and refrigerate overnight or at least 2 to 3 hours before baking. Bake covered at 350 degrees for 50 to 60 minutes or until done.

Mrs. Abner Z. Fisher, Aaronsburg, PA

Mexican Breakfast Casserole

12 eggs, scrambled

1 pound sausage, fried

1½ cups sour cream

1½ cups salsa

1 (10¾ ounce) can cream of mushroom soup

6 tortillas, cut into small squares

Prepare eggs and sausage. In bowl, mix sour cream, salsa, and soup. In 9x13-inch pan, spread half of mixture on bottom. Top with half of tortilla squares then eggs and sausage. Cover with remaining tortilla squares and spread with sour cream mixture. Bake at 350 degrees for about 30 minutes until heated through. This can be prepared and frozen before being baked.

Lela Brenneman, Danville, AL

TATER TOT BREAKFAST CASSEROLE

Tater tots

1 pound bulk sausage, fried

Ham, cubed

8 eggs, scrambled

Shredded cheddar cheese

White sauce (recipe below)

Bacon (optional)

Corn chips, crushed fine

Grease 9x13-inch pan. Layer ingredients in order given. Bake at 350 degrees for 30 minutes or until heated through.

WHITE SAUCE:

2 cups milk

2 heaping tablespoons cornstarch

4 tablespoons butter

½ teaspoon sea salt

¼ teaspoon pepper

1 cup sour cream

In saucepan, stir milk into cornstarch until smooth. Add butter, salt, and pepper. Cook until thickened, stirring constantly. Let boil 1 minute on low heat. Remove from heat. Mix in sour cream.

JULIA TROYER, Fredericksburg, OH

French Toast Casserole

1 cup maple syrup	1 teaspoon vanilla
10 to 16 slices bread	1½ cups milk
5 eggs	¼ teaspoon salt

Pour maple syrup into 9x13-inch pan, coating bottom. Lay bread slices on top. Mix eggs, vanilla, milk, and salt; pour over bread. Refrigerate overnight. Bake covered at 350 degrees for 40 to 45 minutes.

Ruth Ann Yoder, Salisbury, PA

Grits and Ham Casserole

9 cups milk
2¼ cups quick-cooking grits
4½ cups chopped ham
3 cups shredded cheddar cheese
9 eggs, lightly beaten

6 green onions, chopped
1 tablespoon parsley flakes
1½ teaspoons garlic powder
1½ teaspoons salt
¾ teaspoon pepper

In large pot, bring milk to a boil. Stir in grits. Simmer until thick, stirring often for about 5 minutes. Stir in remaining ingredients. Pour into greased 4-quart baking dish. Bake at 375 degrees for 25 minutes until set.

Anna M. Byler, Clymer, PA

Country Brunch Skillet

6 strips bacon
6 cups cubed hash
   brown potatoes
¾ cup green pepper, chopped
½ cup onion, chopped

1 teaspoon salt
¼ teaspoon pepper
6 eggs, beaten
½ cup cheddar cheese, shredded

Cook bacon in large skillet. Remove from pan. Brown potatoes in bacon grease. Add green pepper, onion, salt, and pepper. Stir-fry until almost done; then pour eggs over top. Stir in cheese and cook until done. Crumble bacon on top.

Katie Zook, Apple Creek, OH

Gold Rush Brunch

4 cups cooked and
    shredded potatoes
2 pounds cubed ham
8 scrambled and salted eggs
1 pound shredded
    cheddar cheese
¼ cup butter

¼ cup flour
1¾ cups milk
¼ teaspoon salt
Pepper to taste
1 cup sour cream

Place potatoes in 9x13-inch pan. Layer with ham, eggs, and cheese. In saucepan, melt butter. Stir in flour. Mix well. Add milk, salt, and pepper. Cook until thickened. Add sour cream. Pour over cheese layer and bake at 400 degrees for 30 to 40 minutes. This can be prepared the day before baking.

"This is a favorite for brunch on Christmas Day."

Celesta Schlabach, Millersburg, OH

Breakfast Pizza Delight

1½ pounds sausage
1½ cups pizza sauce
12 slices bread
12 slices cheese

3 cups milk
1 teaspoon salt
5 eggs

In skillet, fry meat, drain fat, and add pizza sauce. In 9x13-inch pan, top 6 slices bread with 6 slices cheese. Add meat mixture, remainder of cheese, and remaining bread. In bowl, beat together milk, salt, and eggs and pour over bread. Bake at 350 degrees for 35 to 45 minutes or until set and golden brown.

Elva Shirk, Dundee, NY

Deluxe Oven-Baked Omelets

6 eggs
1½ cups milk
½ teaspoon salt
1 teaspoon mustard

3 slices bread, cubed
¼ cup chopped onion
1 cup shredded cheese, divided
½ pound sausage, browned

In bowl, beat together eggs, milk, salt, and mustard. Mix in bread, onion, ½ cup cheese, and sausage. Pour into greased 9x9-inch pan. Bake at 350 degrees for 35 minutes. Sprinkle with remaining ½ cup cheese. Bake until just melted.

Martha Beechy, Butler, OH

Omelet Sandwiches

16 slices bread (buttered on one side)
1 pound shaved ham
8 slices cheese
6 eggs

3 cups milk
½ teaspoon mustard
½ teaspoon salt
1 cup cornflakes, crushed
½ cup butter, melted

Make eight sandwiches with bread, ham, and cheese. Put in greased baking dish. Mix eggs, milk, mustard, and salt. Pour over sandwiches. Refrigerate overnight. In the morning, mix cornflakes and butter; sprinkle on top. Bake at 350 degrees for 1 hour. Yields 8 large servings.

Heidi S. Stauffer, Homer City, PA

CREAMED EGGS

6 eggs
6 tablespoons butter
6 tablespoons flour
1½ teaspoons salt
Dash pepper

3 cups milk
4 slices fried bacon, or
  fried sausage or ham
Toast or biscuits

Hard-boil eggs and peel. In heavy saucepan, melt butter and add flour, salt, and pepper. Stir until well blended. Slowly add milk, stirring constantly. Cook until smooth. Chop eggs and crumble bacon. Add to sauce. Serve on toast or biscuits. Yields 6 to 8 servings.

MRS. ALBERT YODER, Stanwood, MI

SCRAMBLED SWEET CORN EGGS

3 ears fresh sweet corn
3 tablespoons butter

4 to 5 eggs, beaten
3 slices American cheese

Remove corn from cob. In skillet, melt butter until lightly browned. Add corn and heat thoroughly. Add eggs and scramble into corn. Cook until eggs are set; top with cheese.

RACHEL STUTZMAN, Dalton, OH

Hidden Eggs

Bread

4 tablespoons butter, melted and divided

6 eggs

Salt and pepper to taste

1 to 2 cups shredded cheddar cheese

In 9x9-inch pan, break up enough bread to cover bottom of pan and drizzle with 2 tablespoons melted butter. Break eggs over bread and sprinkle with salt and pepper. Break up more bread and spread on top of eggs. Drizzle with remaining 2 tablespoons butter and top with shredded cheese. Bake at 350 degrees for 15 to 20 minutes or until eggs are done.

LINDA FISHER, Leola, PA

Simple Cheese Quiche

1 unbaked pie shell

5 eggs

1 cup milk

1 cup cream

1 teaspoon salt

1 teaspoon pepper

½ cup bacon bits

1 cup shredded cheese

Bake pie shell for 10 minutes until lightly browned. Beat eggs, milk, cream, salt, and pepper until well blended. Stir in bacon bits and cheese. Carefully pour into warm pie shell. Bake at 350 degrees for 40 to 50 minutes until quiche is light brown. Allow to cool at least 20 minutes before cutting and serving.

MARTHA BEECHY, Butler, OH

CHEDDAR MACKEREL QUICHE

CRUST:

1 cup flour
¼ teaspoon salt
3 tablespoons cold butter

3 tablespoons shortening
¼ cup milk

In bowl, combine flour and salt. Cut in butter and shortening until crumbly. Stir in milk. On floured surface, roll dough into 10-inch circle. Transfer to ungreased 9-inch pie plate or quiche dish. Trim and flute edges. Bake at 350 degrees for 10 minutes.

FILLING:

1 (15 ounce) can mackerel, drained and deboned
1 cup (4 ounces) shredded cheddar cheese
¼ cup chopped green pepper
¼ cup chopped onion

1 tablespoon flour
½ teaspoon salt
⅛ teaspoon pepper
3 eggs, beaten
1¼ cups milk

In bowl, combine mackerel, cheese, green pepper, onion, flour, salt, and pepper. Spoon into baked crust. Combine eggs and milk; pour over mackerel mixture. Bake at 350 degrees for 50 minutes or until knife inserted near center comes out clean. Let stand for 10 minutes before cutting. Yields 6 servings.

MATTIE PETERSHEIM, Junction City, OH

Easy Veggie Quiche

Vegetables (zucchini, tomatoes, sweet onion), cubed

1 teaspoon salt

Garlic salt, oregano, and basil to taste

2 pounds hamburger, browned and drained

½ cup mayonnaise

½ cup yogurt

1 cup milk

6 eggs, beaten

Shredded cheese

Layer vegetables in 9x13-inch pan. Sprinkle with salt and herbs. Top with hamburger. Mix mayonnaise, yogurt, milk, and eggs together; pour over layered hamburger and vegetables. Bake uncovered at 350 degrees for 1 hour and 15 minutes. Top with cheese during last 10 minutes.

CHRISTINA PEIGHT, Belleville, PA

Breakfast Fried Zucchini

4 cups shredded zucchini
½ teaspoon salt
½ cup milk
2 eggs, beaten

1 cup cracker crumbs
Bacon or ground beef,
cooked (optional)

In skillet, fry salted zucchini until soft. In bowl, combine milk, eggs, and cracker crumbs; add to cooked zucchini. Fry until firm. Add bacon or ground beef if desired.

Mary Zimmerman, Mifflinburg, PA

Syrupy Baked Pancakes and Eggs

1 cup water

⅓ stick butter

¾ cup chicken or beef broth

½ teaspoon stevia powder

1 to 2 tablespoons
   maple flavoring

2 eggs

1 teaspoon salt

4 tablespoons oil

2 teaspoons baking powder

2 teaspoons angel cream
   or cream of tartar

2 cups milk or buttermilk

2 cups all-purpose or
   whole wheat flour

8 eggs

½ cup water

Salt to taste

In saucepan, heat together 1 cup water, butter, broth, stevia, and maple flavoring until butter is fully melted. Pour into 9x13-inch pan. In bowl, blend 2 eggs, salt, oil, baking powder, angel cream, milk, and flour. Pour batter evenly over broth mixture, but do not stir. Bake at 350 degrees for about 30 minutes. In bowl, beat together 8 eggs, ½ cup water, and salt. Pour over hot cake and return to oven for 30 more minutes.

Karen Miller, Monroe, WI

Stuffed French Toast

1 loaf homemade bread
2 (8 ounce) packages
  cream cheese
12 eggs
2 cups milk
½ cup maple syrup

Cinnamon (optional)
2 cups fresh or frozen berries
  (optional for topping)
Chopped nuts (optional
  for topping)

Cube bread and place half in 9x13-inch pan. Cube cream cheese and sprinkle on top. Add remaining bread cubes. In bowl, beat eggs, milk, and syrup and pour over bread. Sprinkle with cinnamon if desired. Let sit for a while to let bread absorb liquid or refrigerate overnight and bake next morning. Bake at 350 degrees for 45 minutes or until golden brown. Serve with maple syrup. Add fruit or nuts as desired for topping.

SADIE ANNE KAUFFMAN, Gordonville, PA

Raspberry Cream Cheese Breakfast Casserole

6 slices bread, broken
into bite-size pieces

1 (8 ounce) package cream
cheese, softened

1 cup raspberries

6 eggs

1 cup milk

¼ cup maple syrup

Put bread into 9x13-inch pan. Beat cream cheese until soft and spread over bread. Sprinkle with raspberries. In bowl, beat eggs; add milk and maple syrup. Pour over raspberries. Bake at 350 degrees for 30 minutes covered and 30 minutes uncovered. Serve warm with milk. This can be made the day before and refrigerated overnight. Take out of refrigerator 30 minutes before baking.

Katelyn Albrecht, Monticello, KY

Apple Oatmeal Pancakes

2 cups buttermilk or sour milk
2 cups old-fashioned oats
2 eggs, divided
¼ cup oil (I use coconut)
½ cup spelt flour
½ teaspoon salt

1 teaspoon baking soda
1 teaspoon baking powder
½ teaspoon cinnamon
2 tablespoons molasses or honey
1 apple, chopped

Start the night before by soaking oats in buttermilk. The next morning, add egg yolks and oil. In separate bowl, combine flour, salt, baking soda, baking powder, cinnamon, molasses, and apple. Gently combine wet and dry mixtures until just moistened. Beat egg whites until stiff and fold into batter. Fry on hot griddle with oil. If batter is too thick, thin with milk.

PHEBE PEIGHT, McVeytown, PA

Baked Oatmeal

2 eggs
½ cup vegetable oil
1 cup sugar
3 cups oats

1 cup milk
2 teaspoons baking powder
Pinch salt

In bowl, mix eggs, vegetable oil, and sugar together. Add oats, milk, baking powder, and salt. Stir until well mixed. Pour into 9x13-inch pan and bake at 350 degrees for 30 minutes. Good served warm with fruit and milk.

Elaine Nolt, Ephrata, PA

Cinnamon Pecan Oatmeal

1¼ cups old-fashioned oats
¼ cup pecans, roasted
2 tablespoons brown sugar

2 teaspoons cinnamon
Pinch salt

Prepare oats according to package directions. Stir in pecans, brown sugar, cinnamon, and salt. Serve with fresh blackberries or additional pecans. It's that simple!

Blueberry Coffee Cake

2¼ cups spelt flour
¾ cup Sucanat or light
  brown sugar
1½ teaspoons baking powder
1½ teaspoons cinnamon
¾ teaspoon salt

2¼ cups fresh or frozen
  blueberries
2 eggs
¾ cup milk
6 tablespoons butter, melted

Topping:
6 tablespoons butter
1½ cups Sucanat

1½ tablespoons flour
¾ cup chopped nuts

In large mixing bowl, combine flour, Sucanat, baking powder, cinnamon, and salt. Gently fold in blueberries. Add eggs, milk, and butter. Spread in greased 9x13-inch pan. Combine topping ingredients and sprinkle over batter. Bake at 350 degrees for 30 minutes or until golden brown.

Rebecca J. Hershberger, Dalton, OH

PLENTIFUL SALADS

For I will pour water upon him that is thirsty, and floods upon the dry ground: I will pour my spirit upon thy seed, and my blessing upon thine offspring.

Cheeseburger Salad

¾ pound ground beef, browned
½ cup chopped dill pickles
¾ cup ketchup
1 tablespoon mustard
Lettuce

Tomatoes, chopped
Onion, chopped
Shredded cheese
Croutons

Mix together beef, pickles, ketchup, and mustard. Layer in bowl starting with lettuce, then beef mixture, tomatoes, onion, cheese, and croutons. Serve with dressing.

Western Dressing:
2 cups Miracle Whip
1½ cups sugar
¼ cup ketchup
½ cup vegetable oil
2 teaspoons mustard

1 teaspoon paprika
4 teaspoons water
½ teaspoon salt
¼ cup vinegar

Mix all together until blended. Very good on taco salad or cheeseburger salad.

Jolene Bontrager, Topeka, IN

White Taco Salad

1 head lettuce, cut up

4 cups cooked and chopped chicken

½ (2.5 ounce) can sliced black olives, drained

2 cups shredded mozzarella cheese

½ bag Ranch Doritos, crushed

1½ (16 ounce) bottles ranch dressing

Mix all together and serve.

Susanna Mast, Kalona, IA

Corn Chip Salad

1 head lettuce, shredded

2 pounds colby cheese, grated

1 bag Fritos corn chips, crushed

2 (15.5 ounce) cans red kidney beans, drained and rinsed

Combine ingredients. Just before serving, pour dressing over and mix in.

Dressing:

1 cup Miracle Whip

⅛ cup vinegar

½ teaspoon paprika

2 teaspoons water

¼ cup oil

¾ cup sugar

¼ cup ketchup

1 teaspoon mustard

¼ teaspoon salt

Blend ingredients together.

Laura Miller, Mount Vernon, OH

Chili Corn Bread Salad

1 (8½ ounce) box corn bread muffin mix

1 (7 ounce) can chopped green chilies, undrained

⅛ teaspoon cumin

⅛ teaspoon oregano

1 cup mayonnaise

1 cup sour cream

1 envelope ranch salad dressing mix

2 (15 ounce) cans pinto beans, drained and rinsed

2 (15¼ ounce) cans whole kernel corn, drained

3 medium tomatoes, chopped

1 cup chopped green pepper

1 cup chopped green onion

10 bacon strips, fried and crumbled

2 cups shredded cheddar cheese

Prepare corn bread batter according to package directions. Stir in chilies, cumin, and oregano. Spread into greased 8x8-inch pan. Bake at 400 degrees for 20 to 25 minutes or until toothpick comes out clean. Cool. In small bowl, combine mayonnaise, sour cream, and dressing mix; set aside. Crumble half of corn bread into 9x13-inch pan. Layer over corn bread with half each of beans, mayo mixture, corn, tomatoes, peppers, onions, bacon, and cheese. Repeat layers once, starting again with corn bread. Dish will be very full. Cover and refrigerate at least 2 hours before serving.

Doretta Yoder, Topeka, IN

Oriental Chicken Salad

1 medium head lettuce, chopped

2 cups chopped grilled chicken breast

1 cup salted cashews

1 (8 ounce) can water chestnuts, sliced

2 cups chow mein noodles

1 small onion, chopped, or 1 tablespoon minced onion

In large bowl, combine salad ingredients.

DRESSING:

½ cup ketchup

¾ cup sugar

¼ cup vinegar

½ cup vegetable oil

1 tablespoon Miracle Whip

2 tablespoons minced onion

1 teaspoon salt

In another bowl, beat together dressing ingredients. Pour over salad and toss just before serving.

LOVINA MILLER, Shipshewana, IN

Bacon Chicken Salad

Dressing:

½ cup mayonnaise

5 tablespoons barbecue sauce

3 tablespoons chopped onion

½ teaspoon salt

1 tablespoon lemon juice

3 tablespoons sugar

¼ teaspoon pepper

¼ teaspoon liquid smoke

Mix together until well blended.

Salad:

4 cups chopped lettuce

4 cups chopped spinach

2 large tomatoes, diced

1½ pounds chicken nuggets, cooked and cubed

10 bacon strips, fried and chopped

2 hard-boiled eggs, chopped

Shredded cheese

Layer first 6 ingredients in order given. Drizzle with dressing and top with cheese.

Jolene Bontrager, Topeka, IN

CHICKEN SALAD

2 cups cubed, cooked chicken

½ cup peeled, seeded, and finely diced cucumber

1 rib celery, finely diced

½ cup dill pickles, drained and finely diced

1 tablespoon grated onion

¾ cup mayonnaise

¼ cup ranch dressing

1 tablespoon parsley flakes

½ teaspoon paprika

½ teaspoon garlic salt

Salt to taste

Mix all together. Add more mayonnaise if you want it more saucy. Serve with crackers or on toast or croissants. This makes a cool meal for hot summer days. Serve with fresh lemonade and watermelon.

KATHRYN TROYER, Rutherford, TN

LETTUCE AND EGG SALAD

1 small onion, chopped

½ cup Miracle Whip

⅓ cup sugar

⅓ cup milk

8 cups chopped leaf lettuce

6 hard-boiled eggs, sliced

Blend onion, Miracle Whip, sugar, and milk. When ready to serve, toss with lettuce and eggs.

EMMA MILLER, Baltic, OH

Egg Salad

3 hard-boiled eggs,
  peeled and chopped

⅛ cup mayonnaise (or more
  if mixture is too dry)

¼ teaspoon vinegar

⅛ teaspoon salt

⅛ teaspoon celery salt

1½ teaspoons mustard

1½ teaspoons sugar

⅛ teaspoon onion salt

In medium-sized bowl, mix chopped eggs with mayonnaise and other ingredients, stirring well. Serve on a bed of lettuce or make a sandwich using fresh bread. A leaf of lettuce, pickles, or sliced olives may be added to the sandwich.

Ham Salad

2 cups chopped potatoes

2 cups macaroni

3½ cups diced ham

3 cups chopped cheese

3 peppers (green, yellow, and orange), chopped

Celery, diced

Pepperoni, chopped

8 ounces sour cream

1 cup Miracle Whip

½ cup mustard

14 ounces heavy cream

Sugar to taste

Salt to taste

In saucepan, cook potatoes and macaroni until tender. Drain and cool. Add ham, cheese, peppers, celery, and pepperoni. In bowl, mix sour cream, Miracle Whip, mustard, and cream. Season with sugar and salt. Pour over salad mixture and stir to coat. The recipe can easily be adapted to your tastes by adding vegetables and seasonings you prefer.

MALINDA HOSTETLER, West Salem, OH

MAKE-AHEAD LAYERED LETTUCE SALAD

1 head iceberg lettuce, chopped

1 head romaine lettuce, chopped

1 small head cauliflower, cut fine

½ pound radishes, sliced thin

Mix together and put in 9x13-inch pan.

TOPPING:

1½ cups mayonnaise

⅓ cup parmesan cheese

¼ cup sugar

1½ cups shredded cheddar cheese

1 pound bacon, fried, drained, and crumbled

Combine mayonnaise, parmesan cheese, and sugar. Spread over vegetables. Top with cheddar cheese and bacon. Refrigerate 24 hours or overnight before serving.

KATHRYN TROYER, Rutherford, TN

Spinach Salad

2 pounds fresh spinach

1 medium onion, finely chopped

4 eggs, hard boiled and diced

6 slices bacon, fried and crumbled

½ pound mushrooms, fresh and sliced

Combine all ingredients. Serve with your favorite dressing.

Lovina Petersheim, Osseo, MI

Delicious Macaroni Salad

6 cups macaroni, cooked

4 eggs, boiled and chopped

2 cups celery, chopped

2 small onions, chopped

2 cups carrots, shredded

2 cups sugar

½ cup vinegar

½ cup water

1 tablespoon mustard

1 tablespoon butter

4 eggs, beaten

1 cup mayonnaise

Combine macaroni, boiled eggs, celery, onions, and carrots in bowl. In sauce-pan, combine sugar, vinegar, water, mustard, butter, and beaten eggs. Boil 2 minutes. Cool. Add mayonnaise. If dressing is too thick when cold, add a little cream to thin it. Stir dressing into salad ingredients until well coated.

Wilma Leinbach, Shippensburg, PA

Pasta Salad

16 ounces spiral pasta, cooked, rinsed, and drained
1 head cauliflower, cut fine

1 large head broccoli, cut fine
1 cup cheese cubes (optional)

In large bowl, combine cooked pasta, cauliflower, broccoli, and cheese.

Dressing:

1 quart mayonnaise
1 package Italian dressing mix

1 package ranch dressing mix

Mix dressing ingredients together and pour over vegetable mixture. If needed, add a bit of sugar and salt. If too dry, add more mayonnaise.

Betty Bricker, Middlefield, OH

Mom's Bean Salad

1 (15 ounce) can green
   beans, drained
1 (15 ounce) can yellow
   beans, drained
1 (15 ounce) can kidney
   beans, drained

1 (10 ounce) box frozen
   lima beans
1 cup carrots, cooked
1 large onion, sliced thin
1 green pepper, cut in strips
3 stalks celery, cut in chunks

In large bowl, mix above ingredients.

Dressing:

2 cups sugar
½ cup water
1½ cups vinegar

½ cup salad oil
1 teaspoon celery seed
1 teaspoon salt

In bowl, mix all dressing ingredients. Wait until sugar is dissolved; then pour over bean mixture. Let stand 24 hours before serving.

Susan Miller, Millersburg, OH

Potato Salad

12 cups cooked and
shredded potatoes

12 eggs, boiled and mashed

½ onion, chopped

2 cups diced celery

1 cup shredded carrots

2 cups mayonnaise

2½ cups sugar

2 teaspoons salt

6 tablespoons mustard

¼ cup vinegar

Mix all together. Makes about 1 gallon.

Esther Burkholder, Sugarcreek, OH

German Salad

4 cups cubed cooked potatoes
¾ quart sliced cooked sausage
6 hard-boiled eggs, sliced

¼ pound butter
1 cup flour
Milk

In bowl, combine potatoes, sausage, and eggs. In skillet, melt butter. Stir in flour and cook until lightly browned. Add milk until a nice sauce forms. Pour over potato mixture and stir to coat.

Mrs. Albert Summy, Meyersdale, PA

Cottage Cheese Garden Salad

4 green onions, finely chopped
6 to 8 radishes, diced
1 green pepper, diced
1 stalk celery, diced
2 carrots, grated

1 tablespoon Miracle Whip
1 (8 ounce) carton
  cottage cheese
Salt and pepper to taste

Mix all ingredients. Serve.

Norma Zimmerman, Latham, MO

Cauliflower Salad

1 head cauliflower,
  separated into florets
1 head lettuce, torn into
  bite-size pieces
9 slices bacon, cooked
  and crumbled

1 large sweet onion, sliced
  and separated into rings
1 cup parmesan cheese, grated
1¾ cups mayonnaise
⅓ cup sugar

In large salad bowl, layer cauliflower, lettuce, bacon, onion, and cheese. Cover and chill several hours. In small bowl, mix mayonnaise and sugar. When ready to serve, pour dressing over salad and toss. Yields 8 to 10 servings.

MARY NEWSWANGER, Shippensburg, PA

Broccoli Strawberry Salad

8 cups broccoli florets
8 ounces swiss cheese,
  cut in ½-inch cubes
2 cups sliced fresh strawberries

¼ cup sliced almonds, toasted
1 cup mayonnaise
2 tablespoons sugar
2 teaspoons apple cider vinegar

In large bowl, combine broccoli, cheese, strawberries, and almonds. In small bowl, blend mayonnaise, sugar, and vinegar. Drizzle over salad and mix.

JOLENE BONTRAGER, Topeka, IN

Broccoli and Cauliflower Salad

1 head broccoli
1 head cauliflower
1 small onion, chopped

6 slices bacon, fried
  and crumbled
2 cups shredded cheese

Cut up broccoli and cauliflower and combine in bowl with onion, bacon, and cheese. Pour dressing over top and stir to coat.

Dressing:

1 cup sour cream
1 cup salad dressing

½ cup sugar
½ teaspoon salt

Mix all ingredients well until smooth.

Rhoda M. Schwartz, Decatur, IN

FRUITED COLESLAW

1 cup chopped unpeeled apple

3 cups shredded cabbage

½ cup drained crushed
  pineapple

¼ cup raisins

½ cup salad dressing

¼ cup pineapple juice

¾ teaspoon celery seed

2 teaspoons sugar

¾ teaspoon mustard

Pinch salt

In large bowl, mix apple, cabbage, pineapple, and raisins. In small bowl, combine salad dressing, pineapple juice, celery seed, sugar, mustard, and salt. Pour over cabbage mixture and stir to coat.

ANITA LORRAINE PETERSHEIM, Fredericktown, OH

Apple Salad

Apples, chopped
½ cup water
½ cup sugar
1 tablespoon butter
1 egg, beaten
1 tablespoon flour

1 teaspoon vinegar
Pinch salt
1 cup whipped topping
Bananas, sliced (optional)
Nuts, chopped (optional)
Mini marshmallows (optional)

Place apples in bowl and sprinkle with some sugar, if you prefer. In saucepan, boil together water, sugar, butter, egg, flour, vinegar, and salt until thickened. Cool and add whipped topping. Pour over apples. Add bananas, nuts, and marshmallows as desired. Do not prepare too far in advance of serving as apples will become brown and mushy.

LEAH KING, Bird-in-Hand, PA

Easy Fruit Salad

2 quarts canned
  peaches, chunked
2 quarts fruit cocktail

1 cup instant lemon
  pudding mix

Drain peaches and fruit cocktail, reserving juice. Mix pudding mix into juice. Add back into fruit. So simple and refreshing.

ANNA M. BYLER, Clymer, PA

Melon Ambrosia

1 cup cubed or balled watermelon

1 cup cubed or balled cantaloupe

1 cup cubed or balled honeydew melon

⅓ cup lime juice

2 tablespoons sugar

2 tablespoons honey

Pineapple (optional)

Fresh mint (optional)

In bowl, combine melon. In small bowl, blend lime juice, sugar, and honey. Pour over melon and toss to coat. Cover and refrigerate for at least 1 hour. Garnish with pineapple or mint if desired.

Mary Ellen Wengerd, Campbellsville, KY

Pots of Soups and Stews

For God is not unrighteous to forget your work and
labour of love, which ye have shewed toward his name,
in that ye have ministered to the saints, and do minister.

Hebrews 6:10

AMISH BEAN SOUP

2 to 3 tablespoons butter
3 quarts milk (approximately)
Salt to taste

8 cups stale homemade
bread cubes
1 cup cooked navy
beans (optional)

Brown butter in saucepan; add milk and bring just to boiling point. Add salt and enough bread to thicken. Cover and let set for 10 minutes before serving. Add beans if desired.

LUCY HACKMAN, Mansfield, OH

Broccoli Cheese Soup

½ cup butter

¾ cup flour

2 quarts milk

2 small heads broccoli,
  cut up and cooked

2 cups cubed processed cheese

1 teaspoon salt

¼ teaspoon pepper

In saucepan, melt butter. Add flour and stir. Add milk, a little at a time, beating with wire whisk until smooth. Add cooked broccoli and bring to boil over low heat, stirring occasionally. Add cheese, salt, and pepper; let stand until cheese is melted. Serve.

Rachel Yoder, Burton, OH

Butternut Squash Soup

2 tablespoons butter

5 cups cubed, peeled winter
   squash (like butternut)

2 cups cubed, peeled potatoes

1 teaspoon salt

½ teaspoon pepper

2 cups diced onion

4 cups chicken broth

1 cup heavy cream

In large pot, melt butter over medium heat. Add squash, potatoes, salt, pepper, and onion. Stir and cook 3 to 4 minutes. Stir in broth. Reduce heat and simmer 20 minutes or until vegetables are tender, stirring occasionally. Blend soup mixture until smooth. Stir in cream and serve.

Anna Zook, Dalton, OH

Chowder

2½ cups chopped carrots

2½ cups chopped celery

2 tablespoons oil or chicken fat

1 tablespoon onion flakes

1 teaspoon garlic salt or ¼
   teaspoon garlic powder

1 tablespoon salt

¾ teaspoon basil

⅓ teaspoon oregano

4 cups cubed potatoes

2 cups chicken broth

In gallon pot, sauté carrots and celery in oil for about 5 minutes. Add seasonings; mix well. Add potatoes. Sauté another 5 minutes. Add broth and cook until potatoes are just getting tender. Turn off heat. Prepare sauce.

Sauce:

1 tablespoon butter

1 tablespoon flour

2 cups milk

4 tablespoons flour

1 teaspoon salt

¼ teaspoon pepper

2 cups diced chicken

1½- to 2-inch slice Velveeta
   cheese, cut up

In saucepan, melt butter; add 1 tablespoon flour, stirring well. In shaker jar, mix milk and 4 tablespoons flour. Add to saucepan and heat to boiling. Reduce heat to low and add salt, pepper, and chicken. Add cheese, stirring until melted and hot. Pour over vegetable mixture in first pot.

ESTHER L. MILLER, Fredericktown, OH

CREAMY VEGETABLE SOUP

2 cups broth or soup stock
¾ cup diced carrots
¾ cup diced potatoes
¾ cup diced celery
½ cup finely chopped onion

2 tablespoons butter
¼ cup flour
Salt and pepper to taste
2 cups milk
½ cup cubed cheese

In stockpot, bring broth to boil. Add carrots, potatoes, and celery. Simmer until tender. In a saucepan, sauté onion in butter, stir in flour, and season with salt and pepper. Gradually add milk. Cook and stir until thickened, then add vegetable mixture. Add cheese; stir until melted.

MRS. ERVIN GIROD, Berne, IN

RIVEL SOUP

1 cup flour
1 egg
1 teaspoon salt

2 tablespoons butter
2 quarts milk

In small bowl, mix together flour, egg, and salt until crumbly rivels form. In saucepan, brown butter. Add milk and bring to boiling. Slowly sprinkle in rivels, stirring constantly. Bring to boil; cook and stir 1 to 2 minutes. Yields 6 servings.

SHARON MISHLER, Lagrange, IN

Potato Soup

2 large potatoes, grated

1 large onion, chopped

2 cloves garlic, minced

2 cups chicken broth

4 cups water

1 pound sausage, browned

½ cup crumbled bacon

Salt, pepper, Italian seasoning, and parsley to taste

1 cup heavy whipping cream

¼ cup fresh parsley leaves

In large pot, place potatoes, onion, garlic, broth, and water, and cook until potatoes are soft. Add browned sausage and bacon. Add spices to taste. Simmer for 10 minutes more. Turn to low heat and add cream. Heat through and serve. Garnish with fresh parsley leaves.

DIANNA YODER, Goshen, IN

CHEESY CHICKEN CHOWDER

2 cups diced potatoes
1 cup diced celery
1 cup diced carrots
½ cup chopped onion
¼ cup butter
⅓ cup flour

1½ teaspoons salt
¼ teaspoon pepper
3 cups chicken broth
2 cups milk
2 cups shredded cheese
2 cups chopped cooked chicken

In pot, boil all vegetables in water until tender. In large pot, melt butter; add flour, salt, and pepper. Stir until bubbly. Add broth and milk; boil until thickened. Add cheese and chicken. Bring to boil. Add vegetables and mix in. Simmer a few minutes.

MARTHA PETERSHEIM, Verdigre, NE

Chicken Corn Soup

1 large chicken
2½ quarts water
4 cups corn

1 package egg noodles
½ teaspoon salt
Dash pepper

In large saucepan, boil chicken in water. When cooked thoroughly, remove chicken, reserving broth. Remove meat from bone and cut into small pieces. Strain broth, then add corn, noodles, chicken, salt, and pepper to taste. Cook until noodles are soft. The amount of noodles added can be adjusted according to the thickness desired. The amount of corn and water can also be adjusted.

MATTIE STOLTZFUS (*THE SIMPLE LIFE*)

Cheddar Ham Chowder

2 cups water

4 teaspoons powdered ham base

2 cups peeled and
cubed potatoes

½ cup diced carrots

¼ cup chopped onion

½ cup sliced celery

1 (16 ounce) can corn
kernels, drained

¼ teaspoon pepper

¼ cup butter

¼ cup flour

1 teaspoon garlic salt

2½ cups milk

2 to 3 cups shredded
cheddar cheese

2 cups cubed ham

10 bacon strips, cooked
and crumbled

In soup pot, bring water and ham base to boil. Add potatoes, carrots, onion, celery, corn, and pepper. Bring to boil; reduce heat and simmer for 8 to 10 minutes or until vegetables are tender. Remove from heat. In medium saucepan, melt butter. Blend in flour and add garlic salt. Slowly add milk, stirring constantly. Cook until thickened. Add cheese; stir until melted. Stir cheese mixture into pot of vegetables. Return soup pot to heat. Add ham and bacon; heat through, stirring occasionally.

Saloma Yoder, Middlefield, OH

Wanda's Hearty Lentil Soup

2 cups dried lentils,
  washed and drained

2 medium carrots, sliced

1 cup chopped cabbage

16 ounces stewed tomatoes

¼ cup chopped onion

1 teaspoon sea salt

½ teaspoon freshly
  ground pepper

8 to 10 cups all-natural
  beef broth

Combine all ingredients in large kettle and cook until vegetables and lentils are tender, about 45 minutes to an hour.

Wanda E. Brunstetter

Split Pea Soup

½ pound green or
  yellow split peas

4 cups water

1 ham hock or meaty ham bone

⅓ cup diced carrots

⅓ cup diced celery

⅓ cup diced onion

½ teaspoon salt

Wash and drain split peas. Note: Split peas do not require soaking. Combine all ingredients in kettle with tight-fitting lid. Bring to boil. Reduce heat and simmer, covered, for 2 hours, stirring occasionally. Remove ham hock or bone. Cool slightly. Cut meat off bone and dice. Add to soup and heat thoroughly.

Sarah Troyer, Mercer, PA

Sauerkraut Soup

1 pound smoked polish sausage,
 cut into ½-inch pieces

5 medium potatoes,
 peeled and cubed

2 medium onions, chopped

2 carrots, cut into ¼-inch slices

3 (14.5 ounce) cans
 chicken broth

1 (32 ounce) can sauerkraut,
 rinsed and drained

1 (6 ounce) can tomato paste

Combine sausage, potatoes, onions, carrots, and chicken broth in large saucepan; bring to boil. Reduce heat; cover and simmer for 30 minutes or until potatoes are almost tender. Don't let them overcook. Add sauerkraut and tomato paste; mix well. Return to a boil. Reduce heat; cover and simmer 30 minutes longer.

CREAMY TURKEY VEGETABLE SOUP

1 cup diced carrots
½ cup diced celery
⅓ cup chopped onion
2 tablespoons butter
2 cups diced, cooked turkey
2 cups water
1½ cups peeled, diced potatoes

2 teaspoons chicken
   bouillon granules
½ teaspoon salt
½ teaspoon pepper
2½ cups milk, divided
3 tablespoons flour

In large saucepan, sauté carrots, celery, and onion in butter until tender. Add turkey, water, potatoes, bouillon, salt, and pepper. Bring to boil. Reduce heat, cover, and simmer for 10 to 12 minutes or until vegetables are tender. Stir in 2 cups milk. In separate bowl, combine flour with remaining ½ cup milk; blend until smooth. Stir into soup. Bring to boil; cook and stir for 2 minutes or until thickened.

EDNA IRENE MILLER, Arthur, IL

Hearty Chicken 'n' Rice Soup

1½ cups chicken broth

3 cups cold water

½ cups uncooked rice

½ cup diced carrots

½ cup diced celery

¾ pound processed cheese, cubed

1½ cups diced cooked chicken

In saucepan, combine broth, water, rice, carrots, and celery; bring to boil. Cover and simmer for 25 minutes. Add cheese and chicken; stir until cheese is melted.

Judith Martin, Millmont, PA

Sausage, Greens, and Potato Soup

1 pound sausage

1 tablespoon oil

3 cloves garlic, minced

1 medium onion, chopped

4 cups chicken broth

2 cups water

2 pounds potatoes,
    peeled and chopped

Salt and pepper

1 cup heavy whipping cream

2 cups chopped greens (spinach,
    kale, lamb's-quarters,
    chard, or dandelion)

In pot cook sausage in oil. When half done, add garlic and onion; cook until browned. Add broth, water, potatoes, salt, and pepper to taste; cook until potatoes are tender. Add cream and greens. Cook until tender and wilted.

Beef and Barley Soup

1¼ pounds steak, cut
  into bite-size pieces
1 tablespoon butter
1 pint beef broth
5 cups water

¾ cup barley
1 (10 ounce) package frozen
  mixed vegetables
Salt and pepper to taste

In large saucepan, sauté steak in butter until browned. Stir in beef broth, water, and barley. Simmer until barley is tender. Stir in mixed vegetables. Cook until just tender. Season with salt and pepper. Serve with crackers.

ANNA M. BYLER, Commodore, PA

Hearty Hamburger Soup

1 pound ground beef
1 cup chopped onion
1 cup chopped green pepper
1 cup sliced carrots
1 cup diced potatoes

3 cups tomato juice
1½ teaspoons salt
½ teaspoon pepper
1 teaspoon chili powder
1 teaspoon Italian seasoning

In large pot, fry beef; add onion and peppers. Fry a couple more minutes. Add carrots, potatoes, tomato juice, salt, pepper, chili powder, and Italian seasoning. Cover and cook until vegetables are tender.

Moses Riehl, Coatesville, PA

Pizza Soup

1 pound hamburger

½ cup chopped onion

¼ cup chopped green pepper

2 cups water

2 teaspoons salt

1 cup diced carrots

1 cup diced potatoes

1 cup dried pasta

4 cups pizza sauce

4 to 6 ounces mushrooms

1 to 3 ounces pepperoni, diced

1 cup peas

Cheese

4 tablespoons butter

In large pot, brown hamburger with onion and green pepper. Add water, salt, carrots, and potatoes. Cook 5 to 10 minutes, then add pasta, pizza sauce, mushrooms, pepperoni, peas, and cheese to your taste. Simmer 30 minutes. Add butter and serve.

LORENE HELMUTH, Junction City, WI

Stuffed Green Pepper Soup

½ cup green peppers, chopped

1 pound ground beef, browned

¼ teaspoon salt

⅛ teaspoon pepper

2 tablespoons parmesan cheese

1 pint tomato juice

⅔ cup rice, cooked

⅛ to ¼ cup brown sugar

Combine all ingredients in large saucepan and cook until peppers are tender.

Wilma Yoder, Dundee, OH

Spaghetti Soup

3 celery stalks, chopped

4 carrots, chopped

½ onion, chopped

1¼ pounds hamburger,
cooked and drained

1 quart tomato juice

¼ teaspoon marjoram

1 teaspoon parsley flakes

1 teaspoon basil

⅛ teaspoon garlic powder

½ teaspoon Italian seasoning

1 tablespoon brown sugar

3 ounces dried spaghetti

Cover vegetables with water, cover, and cook 10 minutes. Add remaining ingredients except for spaghetti, and simmer until vegetables are tender. Break spaghetti into small pieces and cook in water until just tender; drain. Add to soup just before serving. If soup is too strong, add water. The longer it cooks, the better. This soup freezes well.

Esther Schlabach, Vanleer, TN

CAZUELA DE ELSA SOUP

2 medium carrots,
    peeled and sliced
1 medium yellow
    onion, chopped
1 medium sweet potato,
    peeled and cubed
3 pounds cooked chicken, cubed
6 medium cloves garlic, minced

4 teaspoons salt
5 cups water
1 large green pepper,
    cored and sliced
1 medium tomato, chopped
2 ears of corn, sliced from cob
¼ cup cilantro, chopped
Pepper to taste

In tall, narrow stockpot, bring carrots, onion, sweet potato, chicken, garlic, and salt to a boil in water. Lower heat and simmer for 15 minutes. Add green pepper, tomato, and corn. Cover. Bring to boil; lower heat and simmer partially covered for 5 minutes. Stir in cilantro and pepper. Simmer additional 2 minutes. Yields 13 cups.

BARBARA BEECHY, Manawa, WI

TACO SOUP

1 pound ground beef
½ cup chopped onion
⅛ scant cup taco seasoning
1 quart tomato juice
1 pint pizza sauce

1 pint kidney beans or
  refried beans
Shredded cheese
Flavored tortilla chips
Sour cream

In large saucepan, brown beef with onion; drain. Add taco seasoning; stir well. Add tomato juice, pizza sauce, and beans. Simmer for 15 minutes. Serve with cheese, chips, and sour cream.

Lena Troyer, Redding, IA

Summer Garden Chili

1 pound hamburger
2 medium onions, chopped
2 large green peppers, chopped
4 cloves garlic, minced
2 tablespoons oil
½ teaspoon cumin
2 tablespoons chili powder

1 teaspoon oregano
¾ teaspoon salt
2 cans kidney beans
4 large tomatoes, chunked, or
   1 quart canned tomatoes
2 cups water (omit if using
   canned tomatoes)

Brown hamburger in dutch oven. Remove and wipe out grease. Sauté onion, pepper, and garlic in oil over medium heat until soft, about 5 minutes. Add cumin, chili powder, oregano, and salt. Cook 1 minute. Add beans, tomatoes, and water (if using). Bring to boil, reduce heat, and simmer 30 minutes.

Susie Miller, Dundee, OH

Big Batch Texican Chili

1 pound bacon, cut up

3 pounds ground beef

2 medium onions, chopped

1 (6 pound) can stewed tomatoes

1 (106 ounce) can tomato sauce

1 (48 ounce) can tomato juice

2 (15 ounce) cans kidney
  beans, drained and rinsed

4 cups water

4 cups diced carrots

2 cups diced celery

1 cup diced green pepper

3 tablespoons parsley flakes

2 tablespoons chili powder

2 tablespoons salt

½ teaspoon pepper

1 teaspoon cumin

1 package chili seasoning

½ cup brown sugar

In skillet, fry bacon, ground beef, and onions; drain. Transfer meat mixture to large, heavy stockpot. Add remaining ingredients. Bring to boil. Cover and reduce heat to medium low. Simmer 45 minutes. Uncover and simmer 15 minutes. Alternate cooking method: Transfer meat mixture to large slow cooker or small electric roaster; add remaining ingredients. Cover and cook on low heat for 8 hours, stirring occasionally. Can uncover the last hour to help reduce liquid.

Tip: I use the 4 cups water to rinse the tomato cans and be sure I get every bit of tomato into the chili.

Lydia Miller, Loudonville, OH

White Bean Chicken Chili Soup

2 pounds cooked chicken, diced
1 (48 ounce) jar great northern
  beans, undrained
12 ounces shredded
  pepper jack cheese

2 teaspoons cumin
1 (46 ounce) can chicken broth
1 can green chilies (optional)

Combine all ingredients and cook slowly over low heat. Cheese will be less stringy when added to cold ingredients. Serve with sour cream and tortilla chips.

MARY YODER, Millersburg, OH

Dad's Savory Stew

1 pound stew meat, browned

1 cup chopped carrots

1 cup chopped turnips

1 cup chopped celery

1 cup chopped onion

2 cups chopped potatoes

½ teaspoon thyme

½ teaspoon sage

½ teaspoon poultry seasoning

Combine all ingredients in large kettle or dutch oven. Cook 30 minutes or until meat and vegetables are tender. Thicken to your liking with flour and milk. Serve as is or with dumplings, bread, or biscuits.

Wanda E. Brunstetter

Dutch Oven Stew

2 large packages California
   blend vegetables

3 pounds chicken breasts, cubed

1 onion, sliced

1 (16 ounce) bottle
   Italian dressing

1 (16 ounce) bottle
   vinaigrette dressing

Place ingredients in dutch oven. Add water to cover halfway up stew. Bake at 350 degrees with lid on for 50 to 60 minutes until tender. Also can be cooked outside over a campfire.

Susie Hostetler, New Concord, OH

CHILLY DAY STEW

1 large carrot, chopped

3 onions

4 cups peeled and diced potatoes

2 tablespoons rice

2 tablespoons macaroni

1 teaspoon salt

2 cups heavy cream

In kettle ¼ full of water, place chopped carrot. While it starts to cook, chop onions. Add to kettle. Prepare potatoes and add to kettle with rice, macaroni, and salt. Add more water if needed to cover all. Cook slowly until all ingredients are tender. When ready to serve, mix in cream (or substitute a combination of milk and butter). Let heat but do not boil. Serve with crackers or hot toast.

MARY KAUFFMAN, Albion, PA

IDA'S GOOD STEW

Cabbage leaves

Chopped cabbage

Carrots

Green beans

Potatoes

2 packages brats or other meat

Salt and pepper

Put cabbage leaves on bottom of casserole dish. Cut up cabbage, carrots, green beans, and potatoes into bite-size pieces. Cut brats into quarters. Season to taste with salt and pepper. Bake at 350 degrees for 1½ hours in oven or on high in slow cooker.

IDA HOCHSTETLER, Shipshewana, IN

No-Peek Stew

2½ pounds stewing
    beef, cut fine
1 onion, chopped
6 carrots, diced or cut
2 potatoes, cubed

1 teaspoon sugar
1 stalk celery, thickly sliced
2 cups tomato juice
2 teaspoons salt
2½ teaspoons minute tapioca

Place all ingredients in an oven-safe casserole dish. Cover tightly. Bake at 250 degrees for 4 hours. No need to peek at this delicious stew.

Mrs. Jacob Stutzman (*The Simple Life*)

Winter Stew

1 package stew meat
1 to 2 tablespoons flour
1 tablespoon oil
2 cups chopped potatoes
1 cup chopped carrots
1 cup chopped turnips

1 cup chopped celery
1 cup chopped onion
½ teaspoon thyme
½ teaspoon sage
½ teaspoon poultry seasoning

Toss meat in flour to coat. Place meat in large kettle or dutch oven with oil and brown. Cover with water. Simmer for 1½ hours. Add potatoes, carrots, turnips, celery, onions, thyme, sage, and poultry seasoning. Cook 30 minutes more, or until meat and vegetables are tender. Thicken if desired with flour and milk. Serve alone or with biscuits, dumplings, or slices of bread.

Wanda E. Brunstetter

Unique Chicken Stew

4 medium skinless, boneless
  chicken pieces
6 cups cubed potatoes
1 cup sliced carrots
½ cup chopped celery
½ cup chopped onion

2 cups chopped cabbage
4 cups chopped broccoli
3 cups chopped cauliflower
Salt and pepper to taste
Lemon pepper to taste

Dice chicken into 1-inch squares. Place in 6-quart kettle with a little water and cook for 20 minutes. Add potatoes, carrots, celery, onion, cabbage, broccoli, and cauliflower. Add water to almost cover all ingredients. Cook until vegetables are tender. Add salt, pepper, and lemon pepper to taste.

Katie Schmidt, Carlisle, KY

WIENER STEW

6 cups potatoes, diced

3 cups carrots, diced

2 onions, chopped

2 cups celery, diced

2 teaspoons salt

3 pints water

1 pound wieners, sliced

2 tablespoons butter

¼ teaspoon pepper

2 tablespoons flour

1 cup milk

In large pot or dutch oven, cook potatoes, carrots, onions, and celery in salt water until soft. Add wieners, butter, and pepper. Bring to boil. In jar, combine flour and milk and shake or stir to form a smooth paste. Add to stew to thicken broth. Yields 8 servings.

REGINA SCHLABACH, Monticello, KY

DINNERS FROM THE OVEN

And above all things have fervent charity among yourselves: for charity shall cover the multitude of sins.

1 Peter 4:8

Chicken Pie

2 cups chicken broth

2 tablespoons flour

2 cups diced cooked potatoes

2 cups diced cooked carrots

2 cups cooked peas

2 tablespoons chopped
   cooked celery

1 small onion, chopped
   and cooked

2 cups diced cooked chicken

Buttered bread crumbs or
   pie dough rolled out to
   fit oblong baking pan

In saucepan, heat broth. Add 2 tablespoons flour to make a thin gravy. Mix with vegetables and chicken. Pour into 9x13-inch baking pan and cover with bread crumbs or pie dough. Bake at 350 degrees for 1 hour.

Rebekah Mast, Amelia, VA

Impossible Cheeseburger Pie

1 pound ground beef or sausage
½ cup chopped onion
½ teaspoon salt
¼ teaspoon pepper
1½ cups milk

3 eggs
¾ cup Bisquick baking mix
½ pint pizza sauce
1 cup shredded cheese

In large skillet, brown meat and onions. Add salt and pepper, then spread in 9-inch pie pan. Set aside. In bowl, beat milk, eggs, and Bisquick together until smooth. Pour over meat and bake at 400 degrees for 30 minutes or until knife comes out clean. Top with pizza sauce and cheese. Return to oven just long enough for cheese to melt.

CLARA MAST (*THE SIMPLE LIFE*)

POTATO SAUSAGE PIE

3 teaspoons vegetable oil
3 cups shredded raw potatoes
1 cup shredded cheese
¾ cup cooked sausage
¼ cup chopped onion

1 cup milk
2 eggs
½ teaspoon salt
⅛ teaspoon pepper

In bowl, combine oil and potatoes. Press into pie pan. Bake at 425 degrees for 15 minutes or until potatoes begin to brown. Remove from oven and layer potatoes with cheese, sausage, and onion. In bowl, combine milk, eggs, salt, and pepper, and pour over layered ingredients. Bake for 30 minutes or until lightly browned. Cool for 5 minutes before cutting.

ANNIE STAUFFER, Elk Horn, KY

RICE PIZZA

2 cups cooked brown rice

2 tablespoons butter

1 egg, beaten

Baked beans

Mushrooms

Black olives

Shredded cheese

Pizza or Italian seasoning

Mix rice, butter, and egg. Press into bottom of 9x13-inch pan. Top with beans, mushrooms, olives, cheese, and seasoning. Bake at 350 degrees for 30 minutes.

Laura Miller, Mount Vernon, OH

SIMPLE PIZZA RICE CASSEROLE

2 pounds ground beef or turkey

1 teaspoon Italian seasoning

¼ teaspoon garlic powder

1 teaspoon salt

1 pint tomato sauce

1½ cups uncooked brown rice

2 eggs

4 cups water

1 cup chopped onion

Desired toppings (mushrooms, olives, peppers, etc.)

Cheese (optional)

In skillet, brown ground beef. Add Italian seasoning, garlic powder, and salt. Stir in tomato sauce. In greased 9x13-inch pan, spread uncooked rice on bottom. In bowl, mix eggs with water and pour over rice. Distribute meat mixture over rice. Sprinkle onions and other desired toppings over meat. Top with cheese if desired. Bake at 350 degrees for 1¼ hours.

Susanna Mast, Kalona, IA

Vera Mast, Kalona, IA

Upside-Down Amish Pizza

FILLING:

2 pounds ground beef

½ cup chopped onion

Salt and pepper to taste

2 cups pizza sauce

Sliced pepperoni
  pieces (optional)

1 cup chopped green peppers

1 cup chopped mushrooms

16 ounces sour cream

Shredded mozzarella cheese

In skillet, brown meat and onions. Add salt, pepper, and pizza sauce. Pour into 9x13-inch pan. Layer with pepperoni, green peppers, and mushrooms. Bake at 350 degrees for 15 minutes. Remove from oven and cover with sour cream and cheese. Set aside.

TOPPING:

2 eggs

1 cup milk

1 tablespoon oil

½ teaspoon salt

½ teaspoon baking powder

1 cup flour

In bowl, mix all topping ingredients together and put on top of pizza. Bake for 30 minutes or until done.

MRS. JACOB STUTZMAN (*THE SIMPLE LIFE*)

Lazy Wife's Dinner

1 cup diced raw potatoes
1 cup diced carrots
1 cup cooked meat
1 cup uncooked macaroni
3 tablespoons chopped onion

1 can cream of chicken,
   mushroom, or celery soup
1½ cups frozen vegetables
1½ cups milk
1 cup shredded cheese

Combine all ingredients in bowl and pour into baking dish. Cover and bake at 350 degrees for 1½ hours.

Susie Blank, Narvon, PA

Upside-Down Dinner Casserole

½ pound bacon

1½ pounds hamburger

2 medium onions, sliced

1 pound carrots, sliced

Salt to taste

2 tablespoons flour

5 or 6 potatoes, sliced

Salt and pepper to taste

White sauce (recipe below)

Cover bottom of casserole dish with bacon slices. Press hamburger on top of bacon. Follow with layers of onions and carrots. Season with salt. Sift flour over carrots. Layer on potatoes. Season with salt and pepper. Cover with white sauce. Cover and bake at 375 degrees for 1½ hours, until vegetables are tender.

White Sauce:

4 tablespoons butter

4 tablespoons flour

1 teaspoon salt

¼ teaspoon pepper

1 teaspoon parsley flakes

1 teaspoon diced chives

1¼ cups milk

Melt butter in saucepan. Add flour, salt, pepper, parsley, and chives; stir until well blended. Cook for 2 minutes, stirring constantly. Gradually add milk; continue stirring until all milk is incorporated and sauce thickens. Remove from heat.

Edna Irene Miller, Arthur, IL

Deep-Dish Taco Squares

1 pound ground beef
2 cups flour
1 tablespoon baking powder
1 teaspoon salt
⅓ cup margarine
⅔ cup milk

1 cup finely chopped green pepper
2 tablespoons finely chopped onion
1 cup sour cream
⅔ cup mayonnaise or salad dressing
1 cup shredded cheese

In skillet, brown ground beef, drain, and set aside. In bowl, mix flour, baking powder, salt, margarine, and milk. Press into bottom of 9x13-inch pan. Bake at 375 degrees for 15 minutes. Cover crust with beef. Layer on green pepper and onion. Mix together sour cream, salad dressing, and cheese. Pour on top of pan contents. Bake 25 minutes until light brown.

Rebecca Mast, Gambier, OH

Bierock Casserole

2 pounds ground beef
1 onion, chopped
1 head cabbage, shredded
1 can cream of mushroom soup

Salt and pepper to taste
2 cans crescent roll dough
Velveeta cheese, sliced

Brown beef and onion. Drain. Add cabbage and cook until softened. Add soup, salt, and pepper. In greased 9x13-inch pan, cover bottom with contents of 1 can dough. Layer with beef mixture. Cover with cheese slices. Top with remaining dough. Bake at 350 degrees for 1 hour.

Mrs. Orie Detweiler, Inola, OK

Burrito Casserole

2 pounds ground beef, browned

1 (15 ounce) can pork and beans

½ cup brown sugar

1 cup French dressing

1 package taco seasoning

2 (10¾ ounce) cans cream of chicken or mushroom soup

2 cups sour cream

1 package (10 inch) soft tortilla shells

1 (16 ounce) package shredded cheddar cheese

In large bowl, mix together browned beef, beans, brown sugar, French dressing, and taco seasoning. In separate bowl, mix together soup and sour cream; set aside. Put half of soup mixture on bottom of 9x13-inch pan. Layer half of tortillas on top of soup mixture. Put all of beef mixture on top of tortillas. Put remaining tortillas on top. Spread remaining soup mixture over top. Bake at 325 degrees for 1 hour. Remove from oven and top with cheddar cheese; return to oven until cheese is melted.

Leona Mullet, Burton, OH

CHILI PIE CASSEROLE

3 cups corn chips, divided

1 large onion, chopped

1 cup shredded cheese, divided

2 cups chili

Place 2 cups corn chips in casserole dish. Cover corn chips with onion and half of cheese. Pour chili over cheese. Top with remaining corn chips and cheese. Bake at 350 degrees for 15 to 20 minutes.

Sharon Knepp, Chouteau, OK

STUFFED PEPPER CASSEROLE

2 pounds hamburger, browned

1½ cups chopped cabbage

1 large tomato, peeled and chopped

2 large yellow tomatoes, peeled and chopped

1¼ cups uncooked instant rice

1 medium onion, chopped

2 green peppers, chopped

2 red peppers, chopped

2½ cups water

1 tablespoon salt (or to taste)

1 teaspoon pepper

1 cup shredded cheddar cheese

Combine all ingredients except cheese. Pour into baking dish with lid. Top with cheese. Bake covered at 375 degrees for 1½ hours or until rice is tender.

Lucy Zimmerman, Orrstown, PA

BEEF AND NOODLE CASSEROLE

1½ pounds ground beef
1 tablespoon butter
  or margarine
1 large onion, chopped
1 cup green pepper, chopped
1 tablespoon
  Worcestershire sauce

1 (10 ounce) package wide
  noodles, cooked and drained
2 (10¾ ounce) cans cream
  of tomato soup
1 (10¾ ounce) can cream
  of mushroom soup
1 cup (4 ounces) cheddar
  cheese, shredded

In large skillet, brown beef. Remove beef and drain fat; set aside. In same skillet, melt butter over medium-high heat. Sauté onion and pepper until tender. Add beef, Worcestershire sauce, noodles, tomato soup, and mushroom soup. Mix well. Spoon into greased 3-quart casserole dish and top with cheese. Bake at 350 degrees for 45 minutes. Yields 8 servings.

JUDITH MARTIN, Millmont, PA

Country Chicken and Biscuits

3 carrots, sliced
½ cup chopped onion
3½ cups cubed potatoes
2½ cups diced chicken
1 bag frozen peas

1½ cups grated Velveeta cheese
1 to 2 cans cream of
   chicken soup
Milk
Biscuit dough

In saucepan, cook carrots, onion, and potatoes in water until tender; drain. Add chicken, peas, cheese, and soup. Add just enough milk to thin to desired sauce thickness. Bake in covered casserole dish at 375 degrees for 20 minutes until hot and bubbly. Top with biscuit dough and bake uncovered for 20 minutes until golden brown.

Ann Schwartz, Salem, IN

CHICKEN RICE CASSEROLE

4 cups cooked rice
¼ cup melted butter
¼ cup flour
1 teaspoon seasoned salt
¼ teaspoon pepper
2 teaspoons chicken bouillon
½ teaspoon garlic powder
2 cups milk

1 package California blend vegetables, cooked and drained
5 cups diced grilled chicken breast
12 ounces Velveeta cheese
1 cup milk
2 cups sour cream
¼ cup melted butter
1 sleeve Ritz crackers, crushed

Put rice in bottom of 9x13-inch pan. In saucepan, mix ¼ cup melted butter, flour, seasoned salt, pepper, bouillon, garlic powder, and 2 cups milk, and heat until thickened. Pour over rice. Layer on vegetables and chicken. In saucepan, melt cheese in 1 cup milk. Remove from heat; add sour cream. Pour over chicken. Mix ¼ cup melted butter and cracker crumbs. Bake at 350 degrees for 25 to 30 minutes, until heated through.

JOLENE BONTRAGER, Topeka, IN

CHICKEN AND DRESSING

1 chicken, boiled or
baked and deboned

8 to 10 cups bread cubes

2 medium onions, chopped

½ cup shredded carrots or
chopped sweet peppers

½ cup diced celery (optional)

1 teaspoon salt

1 teaspoon pepper

2 teaspoons paprika

1 cup chicken broth

Combine all ingredients in bowl and pour into baking dish. Bake at 300 degrees for 1 hour. Serve with gravy.

LISA MARTIN, Shippensburg, PA

CHICKEN GUMBO CASSEROLE

9 slices bread, cubed

4 cups chopped cooked chicken

¼ cup melted butter

1 cup chicken broth

9 slices Velveeta cheese

1 can cream of mushroom soup

½ cup Miracle Whip

4 eggs, beaten

1 cup milk

1 teaspoon seasoned salt

Combine ingredients in casserole dish. Bake at 350 degrees for 1½ hours. Stir several times while baking.

MRS. AARON (EMMA) GINGERICH, Bremen, OH

Baked Potato Casserole

8 medium potatoes, peeled,
cooked, and cubed

4 tablespoons butter

1 cup sour cream

1 envelope ranch dressing mix

2 cups shredded cheddar cheese

Bacon, crumbled (optional)

Place potatoes in pan with butter. Mix sour cream with ranch dressing mix. Spread over potatoes. Top with cheese and bacon. Bake covered at 350 degrees for 60 minutes.

Esther M. Peachey, Flemingsburg, KY

Chicken Pockets

6 tablespoons melted butter

¼ cup buffalo wing sauce

¼ teaspoon garlic powder

⅛ teaspoon salt

1½ cups shredded
cooked chicken

¼ cup chopped onion

2 (8 ounce) tubes crescent rolls

1 cup shredded cheddar
cheese, divided

Grease 9x13-inch pan and line with parchment paper. In small bowl, mix together butter, wing sauce, garlic powder, and salt. In another bowl, combine chicken, onion, and 3 tablespoons butter mixture. Set aside.

Unroll and flatten crescent dough. Cut each into 8 equal squares. Place some chicken mixture (about 1 tablespoon) in center of each square. Sprinkle with half of cheese. Fold each piece in half to form triangle. Press edges to seal.

Set pockets in baking pan. Drizzle with remaining butter mixture and sprinkle with remaining cheese. Bake at 350 degrees for 30 to 35 minutes until golden brown. Let cool 10 minutes before removing from pan. Serve with ranch dressing.

"This recipe takes a little work, but it's a favorite."

Anna M. Byler, Clymer, PA

CHICKENETTI

6 ounces spaghetti
noodles, cooked

2 cups chicken, cooked
and diced

1 (10½ ounce) can cream
of mushroom soup

2 cups corn

½ cup chicken broth

⅛ teaspoon celery salt

1 teaspoon salt

¼ teaspoon pepper

¾ pound cheese, shredded

Mix all ingredients and put in casserole dish. Bake at 300 degrees covered for 1 hour.

MARY NEWSWANGER, Shippensburg, PA

BARBECUE LOADED BAKED POTATO CASSEROLE

2-pound bag tater tots

¼ cup margarine or butter

Salt and pepper to taste

1 large onion, chopped

1 (2½ ounce) package
bacon bits, divided

3 cups shredded mozzarella
cheese, divided

1 (18 ounce) tub barbecued beef

Coat 9x13-inch pan with cooking spray. Put layer of tater tots in bottom. Slice margarine and lay over tater tots. Sprinkle with salt and pepper. Spread onion, half of bacon bits, and half of cheese on top. Cover with beef. Bake covered with foil at 350 degrees for 45 minutes. Remove from oven and add rest of cheese and bacon bits. Heat until cheese is melted. It is good with ranch dressing.

SHARON KNEPP, Chouteau, OK

Mashed Potato Casserole

¾ cup chopped onion

½ cup butter

8 cups cubed ham (approximately 4 pounds)

3 cups cream of mushroom soup

3 cups cubed Velveeta cheese (1½ pounds)

2 tablespoons Worcestershire sauce

¾ teaspoon pepper

6 quarts mashed potatoes (without any milk or salt)

3 cups sour cream

1 to 2 pounds bacon, cooked and crumbled

Sauté onion in butter; add ham, mushroom soup, cheese, Worcestershire sauce, and pepper. Place in large roaster. Mix mashed potatoes and sour cream; spread on meat mixture. Top with bacon. Bake at 350 degrees for 1 hour.

Sharon Mishler, Lagrange, IN

French Fry Casserole

1 bag frozen french fries, cut smaller

2 cups sour cream

1 package dry ranch dressing mix

1 to 2 cups cooked, chopped chicken

½ cup fried, crumbled bacon

1 cup shredded cheese

In baking dish, place fries. Mix sour cream and dressing mix; pour over fries. Put a layer of chicken over fries, then a layer of bacon and cheese. Bake at 350 degrees for 30 to 40 minutes until done.

Linda Yoder, New Wilmington, PA

TATER TOT CASSEROLE

3 pounds chicken breasts

Salt and pepper to taste

1 can cream of chicken soup

½ cup milk

32 ounces frozen peas

32 ounces tater tots

Velveeta cheese, sliced

Cut up chicken in small cubes. Cook until tender and season with salt and pepper. Mix soup and milk. Add to chicken and pour in bottom of casserole dish. Add peas and tater tots in layers. Bake at 350 degrees for 1½ hours. When heated through, top with cheese slices and return to oven until cheese is completely melted.

ESTHER SCHWARTZ, Harrisville, PA

CHEESY HAM CASSEROLE

½ cup Miracle Whip
1½ cups shredded sharp
  cheddar cheese
1½ cups corkscrew noodles,
  cooked and drained
¼ cup milk

2 cups fresh or frozen
  broccoli florets, chopped
1½ cups chopped ham
½ cup chopped red or
  green pepper
¾ cup seasoned croutons

Mix together ingredients in large bowl. Place in casserole dish. Bake at 350 degrees for 30 to 45 minutes.

VERNIE SCHWARTZ, Stanwood, MI

POTATO STACK CASSEROLE

8 medium potatoes,
  cooked and shredded
1 cup sour cream
1 cup milk
1 package ranch dressing mix

2 pounds ground beef
1 package taco seasoning
3 cups cheese sauce
Nacho-flavored chips

Place potatoes in roaster. Mix sour cream, milk, and ranch dressing mix. Pour on top of potatoes. Brown beef. Add taco seasoning. Put on top of cream layer. Pour cheese sauce over meat layer. Bake at 350 degrees for 30 minutes. Before serving, top with crushed chips.

RUBY BONTRAGER, Lagrange, IN

Scalloped Potatoes and Pork Chops

5 cups peeled and thinly
  sliced raw potatoes
1 cup chopped onion
Salt and pepper to taste

1 can cream of mushroom soup
½ cup sour cream
6 pork loin chops (1 inch thick)
Chopped fresh parsley

In greased 9x13-inch pan, layer half the potatoes and onion and sprinkle with salt and pepper. Repeat layers. In bowl, combine soup and sour cream and pour over potato mixture. Cover and bake at 375 degrees for 30 minutes. Meanwhile, in skillet, brown pork chops on both sides. Place pork chops on top of casserole. Cover and return to oven for 45 minutes or until pork chops are tender. Uncover during last 15 minutes of baking. Sprinkle with parsley. Yields 6 servings.

Mrs. Enos Christner, Bryant, IN

ASPARAGUS PIE

½ pound chopped ham

1 (9 inch) unbaked pie shell

3 cups asparagus pieces

1 cup shredded cheese

Small onion, sliced

3 eggs

1 cup light cream

1 teaspoon salt

Put ham in pie shell; top with asparagus pieces. Sprinkle with cheese and onion. In bowl, beat together eggs, cream, and salt. Pour over asparagus. Bake at 350 degrees for 30 minutes or until set.

RUTH ANN ZOOK, Springs, PA

Broccoli Casserole

Broccoli, chopped in large chunks

Cooked chicken or turkey

2 cans cream of chicken or mushroom soup

1 cup mayonnaise

2 teaspoons lemon juice or vinegar

Salt to taste

Cheese, sliced

Bread crumbs

Cover bottom of 9x13-inch pan with broccoli (can be steamed to soften). Top with cooked chicken. In bowl, blend soup, mayonnaise, lemon juice, and salt. Pour over chicken. Top with cheese then bread crumbs. Bake at 350 degrees for 30 minutes, until browned and bubbly.

Mary Brenneman, Meyersdale, PA

Cabbage Casserole

½ cabbage, medium, finely chopped
Salt to taste
½ cup rice, uncooked

½ cup chopped onion
1 pound ground beef
Salt and pepper to taste
1½ cups tomato juice

Preheat oven to 350 degrees. Spread half of the cabbage in bottom of roasting pan. Sprinkle with salt. Add rice, onion, and meat. Spread remaining cabbage on top. Add salt and pepper to taste. Cover with tomato juice. Bake at 350 degrees for 1½ hours or until done.

MRS. WILLIAM MILLER (*THE SIMPLE LIFE*)

Tomato Pie

CRUST:

⅓ cup milk
¼ cup oil
½ teaspoon salt

1 teaspoon baking powder
1 cup flour

In bowl, thoroughly combine ingredients. Press in 9-inch pie pan. Bake at 375 degrees for 15 minutes.

FILLING:

3 cups peeled, diced fresh tomatoes
½ cup mayonnaise
1 heaping tablespoon brown sugar

1 teaspoon Italian seasoning
Shredded cheese
Diced bell peppers

Combine tomatoes, mayonnaise, brown sugar, and Italian seasoning. Pour in hot crust and top with cheese and bell peppers. Bake for an additional 30 minutes.

KATIE FISHER, Aaronsburg, PA

Tex-Mex Summer Squash Casserole

7 medium yellow squash
or zucchini, sliced
(about 10 cups)

2¼ cups shredded cheddar
cheese, divided

1 medium red onion, chopped

1 (4 ounce) can chopped
green chilies

1 small can diced jalapeño
peppers, drained

¼ cup flour

½ teaspoon salt

¾ cup salsa

4 green onions, sliced

¼ cup chopped red onion

In large bowl, combine squash, ¾ cup cheese, red onion, chilies, and jalapeños. Sprinkle with flour and salt; toss gently to combine. Transfer to greased 9x13-inch dish. Bake covered at 400 degrees for 30 to 40 minutes or until squash is tender. Spoon salsa over top, sprinkle with remaining cheese. Bake uncovered for 10 to 15 minutes or until golden brown. Let stand 10 minutes. Top with green onions and ¼ cup chopped red onion. Yields 10 servings.

Mary Yoder, Millersburg, OH

Summer Zucchini Casserole

⅓ cup olive oil

2 tablespoons wine vinegar

2 tablespoons parsley

3 teaspoons salt

¾ teaspoon pepper

1 teaspoon hot sauce

1 medium zucchini, chopped

2 white potatoes, chopped

2 small green peppers, chopped

2 carrots, chopped

1 celery stalk, chopped

3 to 4 medium tomatoes, sliced thin, divided

½ cup uncooked rice (not instant)

1¾ cups shredded cheddar cheese

Blend oil, vinegar, parsley, salt, pepper, and hot sauce; set aside. Mix zucchini, potatoes, peppers, carrots, and celery in large bowl. Spray large casserole dish with oil. Cover bottom with layer of sliced tomatoes. Cover with half the vegetables. Place another layer of tomatoes. Sprinkle with rice. Add remaining vegetables and top with final layer of tomatoes. Stir oil mixture and pour over all. Cover with foil and bake 1¼ hours at 350 degrees. Remove foil and sprinkle with cheese. Bake another 15 minutes.

Zucchini Lasagna

1 pound ground beef or turkey

¼ cup chopped onion

1 (15 ounce) can tomato sauce

1 teaspoon sea salt

½ teaspoon oregano

½ teaspoon basil

¼ teaspoon pepper

4 medium zucchinis

1 cup regular or low-fat cottage cheese

1 egg, beaten

3 tablespoons gluten-free flour or thickener of choice, divided

Sea salt

2 cups shredded part-skim mozzarella cheese, divided

In skillet, brown beef and onions. Add tomato sauce, salt, oregano, basil, and pepper. Bring to boil. Simmer 5 minutes. Slice zucchini lengthwise into ¼-inch slices. In small bowl, combine cottage cheese and egg. Place half of zucchini slices in 9x13-inch pan. Sprinkle with half of flour and additional salt. Top with cottage cheese mixture and half of meat. Layer on remaining zucchini slices and flour, and sprinkle with salt. Spread with 1 cup mozzarella cheese and top with remaining meat. Bake covered at 375 degrees for 1 hour until heated through and zucchini is tender. Remove cover and top with remaining 1 cup mozzarella cheese. Return to oven until cheese is melted.

EDNA IRENE MILLER, Arthur, IL

Layered Dinner

1½ pounds ground beef
Salt and pepper to taste
¼ cup ketchup
1 head cabbage

6 to 8 cups diced potatoes
4 slices cheese
1½ cups milk

In skillet, brown ground beef. Season with salt and pepper. Mix in ketchup. Set aside. Shred ½ head of cabbage into large baking dish. Add half of potatoes. Sprinkle with salt and pepper. Add all of the beef. Cover with cheese slices. Shred remaining cabbage over cheese. Add remaining potatoes. Pour milk over all. Bake at 375 degrees for 1½ to 2 hours.

Anna M. Byler, Clymer, PA

Overnight Casserole

2 cups meat (chicken, ham, or beef)
2 cups milk
2 cups uncooked macaroni

2 cans cream of chicken soup
½ pound diced Velveeta cheese
1 cup peas

Mix and let sit overnight in refrigerator. Bake in 9x13-inch pan at 350 degrees for 1 hour.

Amanda Rose Esh, Parkesburg, PA

3 Bean Bake

1 (16 ounce) can lima beans, drained

1 large can pork and beans, drained

1 (16 ounce) can kidney beans, drained

2 medium onions, finely chopped

½ pound bacon, fried and crumbled; or chopped hot dogs; or ground beef, fried

¾ cup brown sugar

¾ cup ketchup

1 tablespoon mustard

Place beans, onions, and meat in dutch oven. Mix brown sugar, ketchup, and mustard. Pour over beans and mix in. Bake at 275 degrees for 1 hour.

Iva Troyer, Apple Creek, OH

Good Baked Beans

2 quarts cooked navy beans

2 cups brown sugar

¼ cup water

2 teaspoons salt

2 teaspoons onion salt

2 teaspoons liquid smoke

4 tablespoons minced onion

2 tablespoons butter

6 tablespoons bacon grease

1 quart crumbled fried bacon

Mix everything together. Bake at 375 degrees for 1 hour or cook in slow cooker on high heat for 4 to 5 hours.

Mrs. Reuben (Martha) Byler, Atlantic, PA

Ozark Baked Beans

2 pounds ground beef,
  browned and drained

2 pounds bacon, chopped, fried,
  and drained (reserve grease)

4 (15 ounce) cans kidney
  beans, partially drained

4 (15 ounce) cans lima
  beans, partially drained

4 (15 ounce) cans pork and
  beans, partially drained

4 cups chopped onion

1⅓ cups sugar

1½ cups brown sugar

½ cup molasses

1 cup ketchup

1 cup barbecue sauce

¼ cup mustard

4 teaspoons chili powder

2 teaspoons salt

½ teaspoon pepper

Mix all together in roasting pan, adding some reserved bacon grease if desired. Bake at 350 degrees for 1 hour.

Mary Ellen Wengerd, Campbellsville, KY

Spaghetti Corn

1 cup dried spaghetti, broken

2 to 4 cups corn

1 cup milk

2 cups cooked meat
  (hamburger, ham, chicken)

1 cup grated cheese

Salt and pepper to taste

Mix all ingredients in casserole dish, cover, and bake at 350 degrees for 1 hour.

Mrs. Peter Landis, Brodhead, WI

Zippy Vegetable Casserole

3 cups seeded and chopped
   fresh plum tomatoes

3 cups chopped zucchini

1 green pepper, chopped

½ teaspoon parsley flakes

½ teaspoon basil

¾ teaspoon garlic salt

1 cup shredded
   mozzarella cheese

2½ cups bread crumbs

4 tablespoons butter, melted

Coat 9x13-inch dish with nonstick vegetable spray. Place tomatoes, zucchini, and green pepper in baking dish. Sprinkle with parsley flakes, basil, and garlic salt. Mix together cheese, bread crumbs, and butter. Toss 1½ cups crumb mixture with veggies. Pour remaining crumbs over top of veggies. Bake at 350 degrees for about 45 minutes.

Note: Make ahead of time and store in refrigerator up to 24 hours before baking.

Esther M. Peachey, Flemingsburg, KY

PIGS IN THE GARDEN

1½ pounds raw smoked sausage
   links, cut in 1-inch chunks

5 large potatoes, thinly sliced

2 to 3 carrots, cut in
   3-inch sticks

2 cups fresh green beans

1½ cans cream of
   mushroom soup

¾ cup milk

Salt and pepper to taste

Velveeta cheese, sliced

Arrange sausage to cover bottom of 2-quart casserole dish. Layer vegetables over sausage. Mix together soup, milk, salt, and pepper. Pour over vegetables. Cover with cheese slices. Cover and bake at 350 degrees for 1½ to 2 hours.

ANITA LORRAINE PETERSHEIM, Fredericktown, OH

HOT DOG SURPRISE

1 teaspoon chopped onion

2 cups chopped hot dogs

2 cups chopped ham

½ cup grated cheese

2 hard-boiled eggs, chopped

2 tablespoons pickle relish

3 tablespoons ketchup

1 teaspoon mustard

3 tablespoons mayonnaise
   (optional)

Hot dog rolls

In large bowl, mix all ingredients except rolls. Put mixture in rolls. Wrap in foil and bake at 350 degrees for 12 minutes.

FEENIE BEILER, Delta, PA

GARDEN VEGGIE CASSEROLE

Zucchini, sliced
Sweet corn, cut off cob
Carrots, sliced
Green beans, cut up
1 cup sour cream

1 can cream of chicken soup
½ cup cheddar cheese sauce
1 box chicken-flavored
 dressing mix

Layer vegetables on bottom of small roaster pan. Mix together sour cream, soup, and cheese sauce. Spread over vegetables. Prepare dressing according to box and place on top of sauce. Cover and bake at 350 degrees for 30 minutes. Uncover and bake for 15 to 20 minutes until browned and done.

FREEMAN AND LINDA MILLER, Spartansburg, PA

Ham and Cheese Sticky Buns

1 (12 count) package whole
  wheat dinner rolls

½ pound sliced ham

1 pound swiss cheese

¼ cup butter

2 tablespoons
  Worcestershire sauce

2 tablespoons poppy seeds

2 tablespoons prepared mustard

⅓ cup brown sugar

Remove dinner rolls from package without breaking apart individual rolls. Slice whole group of rolls in half and set bottom half in greased 9x13-inch pan. Layer with ham and cheese. Cover with top layer of rolls. In saucepan, combine butter, Worcestershire sauce, poppy seeds, mustard, and brown sugar until dissolved into a sauce. Pour over and between rolls. Bake covered with foil at 350 degrees for 10 minutes. Uncover and bake 10 more minutes. Slice apart and serve.

Arlene T. Miller, Sugarcreek, OH

Spicy Sandwich Loaf

1 tablespoon butter
1 cup sliced mushrooms
½ cup chopped green pepper
1 pound frozen bread
  dough, thawed
4 ounces ham, thinly sliced

4 ounces salami, thinly sliced
4 ounces shredded
  mozzarella cheese
1½ ounces pepperoni,
  thinly sliced

In large skillet, melt butter. Add mushrooms and peppers; cook, stirring often, until tender. Set aside. On large baking sheet lined with aluminum foil, press dough into 10x13-inch rectangle. Layer ham, salami, cheese, and pepperoni down center of dough. Top with mushrooms and peppers. Fold sides of dough, overlapping edges. Turn seam-side down and pinch ends together. Let rise for 1 hour. Bake at 350 degrees for 30 to 40 minutes until golden brown. Good served hot or cold.

Betty Bricker, Middlefield, OH

Stovetop Suppers

As ye have therefore received Christ Jesus the Lord, so walk ye in him: Rooted and built up in him, and stablished in the faith, as ye have been taught, abounding therein with thanksgiving.

Colossians 2:6–7

Cowboy Hash

2 pounds ground beef

1 cup pork and beans

1 cup ketchup

4 cups mixed vegetables

4 tablespoons mustard

¼ cup brown sugar

In skillet, brown beef. Stir in beans, ketchup, vegetables, mustard, and brown sugar.

Heat thoroughly. Good served with corn bread.

Mary Petersheim, Apple Creek, OH

Woodchopper's Hash

2 tablespoons shortening

5 medium potatoes, peeled and diced

1 quart green beans, drained

½ cup chopped onion

3 slices bread, cubed

4 eggs, beaten

In large skillet, melt shortening. Fry potatoes until soft. Add beans, then onions and bread. Fry until done, then add eggs without stirring. Cook a few minutes, until eggs are set, then turn to light brown.

Mrs. William Miller (*The Simple Life*)

Farmer Yoder's Skillet Supper

2 pounds ground beef

1 medium onion, chopped

3 tablespoons liquid
    aminos or soy sauce

1 tablespoon butter

1 (12 ounce) package frozen
    mixed vegetables

1 cup instant brown rice

5 eggs, beaten

Salt and pepper to taste

In large skillet, brown beef and onion; drain. Add liquid aminos and butter. Mix in vegetables. Cook until soft. Cook rice according to package directions. Add to beef mixture. Pour eggs over mixture. Stir-fry until eggs are well done. Add salt and pepper as desired.

Karen Yoder, Sugarcreek, OH

GARDEN SKILLET

2 pounds ground bulk sausage
5 medium red potatoes, sliced
4 medium carrots, sliced
3 medium zucchini, sliced
4 cups cut green beans
1 medium onion, chopped

1 medium tomato, cut
  into wedges
1 red or green pepper, chopped
1 teaspoon Accent
Salt and pepper to taste

In large skillet, fry sausage until no longer pink. Add potatoes and carrots; cook 5 minutes. Then add remaining vegetables and seasoning. Steam until all are tender.

REBECCA T. CHRISTNER, Bryant, IN

SOUTHWEST SKILLET SUPREME

2 pounds ground beef
1 teaspoon oregano
1 teaspoon salt
2 teaspoons chili powder
1 (16 ounce) can refried
  or pinto beans
3 (15 ounce) cans tomato sauce

1½ cups shredded
  cheddar cheese
Tortilla chips
2 cups shredded lettuce
2 tomatoes, diced
1 (4 ounce) can sliced
  black olives, drained
Sour cream

In large skillet, brown meat. Add oregano, salt, chili powder, beans, and tomato sauce. Simmer 5 to 10 minutes. Pour onto large serving tray. Sprinkle on cheese. Arrange chips around edge of serving tray. Garnish with lettuce, tomatoes, olives, and small dollops of sour cream. Serves 8.

DIANA MILLER, Fredericktown, OH

SAUSAGE SQUASH SKILLET

1 pound sausage, sliced
3 tablespoons chopped onion
3 medium yellow squash, sliced

Seasoning of your choice
Cheddar cheese, shredded

In skillet, fry sausage and onions until sausage is almost cooked through. Add squash and sauté until squash is soft, about 10 minutes. Season and sprinkle with cheese. Let melt before serving.

NORMA YUTZY, Drakesville, IA

SKILLET SQUASH DINNER

½ stick butter, plus
   more if needed
½ pound hamburger
1 large onion, chopped

1 butternut squash, thinly
   sliced or diced
Salt and pepper to taste
Cheese, shredded

In skillet, melt butter and add hamburger, onion, and squash. Cover tightly with lid. Stir every 5 minutes until done. More butter may be needed. Add salt and pepper. Sprinkle with cheese and cover skillet until it melts. Serve immediately.

MARY ANN YUTZY, Bloomfield, IA

Zucchini Skillet Supper

1 medium zucchini
½ stick butter
1 medium tomato, diced
1 small onion, diced
Leftover meat (sausage,
    hamburger, or other)

1 (8 ounce) can
    mushrooms, drained
16 ounces salsa
16 ounces sour cream
Seasoned salt to taste
2 cups shredded cheese

Peel and grate zucchini. Heat large skillet; add butter. After butter is melted, add zucchini, tomato, onion, meat, and mushrooms. Stir well. Add salsa and sour cream, mixing well. Season with seasoned salt. Stir periodically until thoroughly hot. Top with shredded cheese.

EllaMae Hilty, Berne, IN

Six-Layer Dinner

Bacon slices

1 to 1½ pounds
   hamburger, browned

6 medium potatoes, sliced

1 to 2 onions, sliced

Salt

Peas

Carrots

Mushrooms

Shredded cheese

In 6-quart kettle, line bottom with bacon topped with hamburger. Add layers of potatoes and onion. Sprinkle with salt. Add your choice of vegetables. Start burner on high to fry bacon at bottom of pot. Lower heat, cover, and cook until potatoes and vegetables are tender when pierced by a fork. Do not stir. Top with cheese. Delicious and easy!

Mrs. Paul Schrock, Salem, MO

GOULASH

2 pounds ground beef

1½ cups chopped onion

1 green sweet pepper, chopped

1 clove garlic, minced

2 cups macaroni, cooked
  and drained

2 to 3 tablespoons chili powder

Salt and pepper to taste

½ teaspoon garlic powder

2 (16 ounce) cans chili beans

2 (14.5 ounce) cans
  diced tomatoes

2 to 3 cups tomato juice

In stockpot, cook ground beef, onion, pepper, and garlic; drain. Add remaining ingredients. Cook over low heat, allowing to simmer for 20 to 30 minutes until all flavors combine.

Amish Beef Stroganoff

2 tablespoons butter
1 pound ground beef
½ cup diced onion
1 tablespoon garlic salt
1 tablespoon flour
1 can cream of chicken soup

1 (4 ounce) can mushrooms, undrained
1 teaspoon salt
¼ teaspoon pepper
1 cup sour cream
Noodles, cooked

In large skillet, melt butter. Add ground beef, onion, and garlic salt and cook until meat is done. Stir in flour. Add soup, mushrooms, salt, and pepper. Heat through, then add sour cream. Serve over noodles.

BLT Stir-Fry

Equal parts garden vegetables
  (green beans, summer squash,
  tomatoes, zucchini, etc.)

1 stick butter

Cooked meat of your choice
  (chicken breast is good)

Put vegetables in large saucepan and add butter. Simmer on low heat until softened. Add meat; heat through. Serve with BLT dressing.

BLT Dressing:

2 cups ranch dressing

4 tablespoons barbecue sauce

2 teaspoons vinegar

2 teaspoons sugar

Mix all ingredients well.

Miriam Byler, Hartstown, PA

Chicken Stir-Fry

2 cups chopped broccoli
2 cups chopped cauliflower
2 cups sliced carrots
2 cups chopped green beans

2 cups chunked cooked chicken
Salt and pepper to taste
1 can cream of mushroom soup
Shredded cheese

In large skillet, cook vegetables and chicken until vegetables are tender and chicken is no longer pink. Season with salt and pepper. Stir in soup and cheese.

Mrs. Samuel J. Schwartz, Bryant, IN

Summer Stir-Fry

2 tablespoons butter
1 cup shredded zucchini
Leftover boiled or fried potatoes
Chopped onion

6 eggs, beaten
Cheese, shredded
Tomatoes, chopped
Green peppers, chopped

Melt butter in large frying pan; add zucchini, potatoes, and onion. Cook until onion is tender. Add eggs; scramble. When eggs are cooked, top with cheese. Serve with topping of tomatoes and green pepper.

Mary Grace Peachey, Catlett, VA

Green Bean Meal

3 pounds chunked ham

Small early potatoes
with skins on

Fresh green beans, snapped

In an 8-quart kettle, put ham on bottom. Top with layer of potatoes then green beans. Fill pot three-quarters full of water. Cook until tender.

"This is one of our favorite summer meals."

Anna Byler, Spartansburg, PA

Favorite Green Beans

1 pound ground beef

2 tablespoons chopped
fresh garlic

½ cup chopped onion

2 to 3 pounds fresh green
beans, snapped

1 teaspoon paprika

1 teaspoon salt

½ cup ketchup (optional)

4 ounces cream cheese
(optional)

In heavy saucepan, brown beef, garlic, and onion with lid on. Add green beans, paprika, and salt. Slowly simmer until beans reach desired tenderness. May need to add water. For a creamy zest, add ketchup and cream cheese.

Norma Yutzy, Drakesville, IA

Grandma's Cabbage

1 pound sausage   Seasoned salt
½ head cabbage, shredded

Brown sausage; add cabbage and brown lightly. Season to taste with seasoned salt. Cover and steam cabbage for 15 minutes. To serve, drizzle with ranch or your favorite dressing.

Luella Miller, Shreve, OH

Curry and Rice

2 tablespoons olive oil

1 clove garlic, minced

1 teaspoon grated ginger

3 boneless, skinless chicken breasts, cut into bite-size pieces

1 (13.5 ounce) can unsweetened coconut milk

2 to 4 tablespoons red curry paste

¾ cup chicken broth

5 ounces snow peas, chopped

2 lemongrass stalks, bruised

Salt and pepper to taste

1 tablespoon chopped cilantro

Cooked rice

In large skillet, heat olive oil and stir-fry garlic and ginger for 30 seconds. Turn down heat to medium high and add chicken. Cook 5 minutes until chicken is no longer pink. Stir in coconut milk, curry paste, chicken broth, peas, and lemongrass. Bring to boil. Reduce heat and simmer for 10 minutes. Remove lemongrass. Season with salt and pepper. Garnish with cilantro. Serve over rice.

Loretta Petersheim, Mifflin, PA

DANDELION GRAVY

3 to 4 slices bacon
½ cup chopped onion
2 tablespoons flour
1 cup milk
1 tablespoon vinegar (optional)

2 hard-boiled eggs, chopped
Salt and pepper
2 to 3 cups chopped tender
  spring dandelion leaves
  (before it flowers)

Fry bacon and onion in skillet until bacon is crisp and onions are browned; set aside, reserving bacon grease in skillet. Add flour to grease. Cook gently until lightly browned. Slowly add milk, stirring until smooth and thickened. Add vinegar, eggs, bacon, and onions. Season to taste with salt and pepper. Add dandelion leaves. As soon as leaves wilt, gravy is ready. Can be served on toast or with mashed or fried potatoes.

Quick Jambalaya

1 tablespoon oil
½ cup chopped onion
½ cup chopped green pepper
2 cups cooked, chopped chicken
2 cups cooked rice or macaroni
1 (15 ounce) can kidney
    beans, drained and rinsed

1 cup salsa
1 teaspoon thyme
1 teaspoon salt
½ teaspoon pepper
Shredded cheese

Heat oil in skillet. Fry onion and pepper until tender. Add chicken, rice, kidney beans, salsa, thyme, salt, and pepper. Simmer 15 minutes. Top with cheese and serve.

SALOMIE E. GLICK, Howard, PA

Spanish Rice

1 cup rice	1 teaspoon salt
1 pound ground beef	Dash pepper
1 onion, chopped	3 cups tomato juice

In saucepan, cook rice until tender. Brown beef in skillet with onion. Add salt and pepper to beef. Add tomato juice and rice. Simmer until juice is reduced.

Mrs. Albert Summy, Meyersdale, PA

German Pizza

1 pound ground beef, browned
½ medium onion, chopped
½ green pepper, diced
1½ teaspoons salt, divided
½ teaspoon pepper
2 tablespoons butter

6 raw potatoes, shredded
3 eggs, beaten
⅓ cup milk
2 cups shredded cheddar
  or mozzarella cheese

In 12-inch skillet, brown beef with onion, green pepper, ½ teaspoon salt, and pepper. Remove beef mixture from skillet; drain skillet and melt butter. Spread potatoes over butter and sprinkle with remaining 1 teaspoon salt. Top with beef mixture. In bowl, combine eggs and milk, and pour over all. Cook, covered, on medium heat until potatoes are tender, about 30 minutes. Top with cheese; cover and heat until cheese melts, about 5 minutes. Cut into wedges or squares to serve.

Sloppy Bar-B-Q

2 pounds ground beef

¼ cup minced onion or ¼ teaspoon onion powder

2 teaspoons salt

¼ teaspoon pepper

2 tablespoons brown sugar

½ cup ketchup

1 tablespoon mustard

2 tablespoons flour

½ cup water

In skillet, fry ground beef with onion, salt, and pepper. Add brown sugar, ketchup, and mustard. Mix flour and water; add to beef mixture to thicken. Serve on hamburger buns.

Mary K. Bontrager, Middlebury, IN

Sloppy Sandwiches

1 pound hamburger

½ small onion, chopped

½ teaspoon garlic, minced

1 (10 ounce) can condensed cream soup (chicken, mushroom, or celery)

12 hamburger buns

In skillet, brown hamburger, onion, and garlic. Add soup and simmer until thickened. Serve on buns or bread.

Barbecue Ham Sandwiches

1 cup ketchup

3 tablespoons lemon juice

¼ cup chopped onion

¼ cup brown sugar

2 tablespoons
Worcestershire sauce

1 teaspoon mustard

Celery, chopped (optional)

2 pounds chipped ham slices

In saucepan, combine all but ham. When hot, add ham and heat through. Serve on buns. Good for crowds. (5 pounds ham will fill 60 buns.)

ALMA GINGERICH, Irvona, PA

Taco Burgers

1 pound ground beef

1 teaspoon chili powder

¾ teaspoon garlic salt

½ teaspoon sugar

1½ cups tomato juice

1 teaspoon Worcestershire
sauce (optional)

¼ teaspoon dry mustard

8 hamburger buns

2 cups shredded lettuce

1 cup shredded cheese

Chopped tomatoes

In large skillet, brown beef; drain. Add chili powder, garlic salt, sugar, tomato juice, Worcestershire sauce, and dry mustard. Simmer uncovered for 15 to 20 minutes or until thick. Spoon on toasted buns. Sprinkle with lettuce, cheese, and tomatoes. You can use any vegetables you want.

LIZZIE YODER, Fredericksburg, OH

CORN FRITTERS

1 pint sweet corn (fresh, frozen, or canned and drained)
½ cup flour
¼ cup crushed cracker crumbs
½ teaspoon baking soda
½ teaspoon pepper
1 teaspoon salt
1 egg, beaten
¼ to ½ cup milk
Lard or oil

Combine first 7 ingredients along with just enough milk to make it hold together but not be too runny. Drop by tablespoonfuls onto hot griddle greased with lard. Fry on both sides. Good served with applesauce or tomatoes.

RACHEL YUTZY, Nickerson, KS

POTATO PANCAKES

3 cups shredded potatoes
2 eggs, beaten
1½ tablespoons flour
⅛ teaspoon baking powder
1 teaspoon salt
Oil or butter

Combine potatoes and eggs; stir in dry ingredients. Fry in hot oil as you would for pancakes.

LAURA HERSHBERGER, Howard, OH

Tomato Fritters

2 cups canned or fresh
   tomatoes, diced or mashed

2 eggs, beaten

2 tablespoons margarine,
   melted

½ teaspoon salt

2 tablespoons tomato juice

½ cup plus 2 tablespoons flour

Margarine or oil for frying

Combine tomatoes and egg; mix in margarine and salt. Stir in tomato juice, then flour until there are no lumps. Melt margarine in frying pan. Pour batter into pan in pancake-sized fritters. Fry until tops and edges are covered with bubbles and edges are browned. Flip and cook until browned.

Mary H. Miller, Heuvelton, NY

Zucchini Fritters

3 cups grated zucchini

2 eggs

2 tablespoons flour

½ teaspoon salt

1 medium onion, chopped fine,
   or ½ teaspoon garlic powder

½ cup grated cheese (optional)

Mix well. Drop by tablespoonfuls onto well-greased skillet on medium heat. Fry until golden brown; turn and fry other side. Delicious on sandwiches with tomatoes, onions, cheese, etc. Or serve with ketchup or salsa.

Henry and Fannie Hertzler, Bloomsburg, PA

EASY DESSERTS

Blessed be the Lord, who daily loadeth us with benefits.

PSALM 68:19

ALMOST CANDY BARS

1½ cups flour

½ cup cocoa powder

¾ cup powdered sugar

1 cup butter

8 ounces chocolate chips

8 ounces butterscotch chips

1 cup shredded coconut

1 (14 ounce) can sweetened
condensed milk

Mix together flour, cocoa powder, powdered sugar, and butter. Press into 9x13-inch pan. Sprinkle with chocolate chips, butterscotch chips, and coconut. Drizzle with milk. Bake at 350 degrees for 20 minutes.

MRS. JOHN H. MULLET, Cass City, MI

Apple Butter Bars

1½ cups flour
1 teaspoon soda
1 teaspoon salt
2½ cups oats

1½ cups sugar
1 cup margarine
1½ cups apple butter

In large bowl, sift together flour, soda, and salt. Add oats and sugar. Stir in margarine and mix well. Press half of mixture in bottom of greased 9x13-inch pan. Top with apple butter. Sprinkle with remaining crumbs; press gently with spoon. Bake at 350 degrees for 55 minutes or until brown.

NELSON AND MIRIAM HERSHBERGER, Calhoun, IL

Coffee Bars

2⅔ cups brown sugar
1 cup vegetable oil
1 cup warm coffee (made with
    1 teaspoon instant coffee)
1 teaspoon salt
1 teaspoon soda

1 teaspoon vanilla
2 eggs
3 cups flour
1 cup nuts, chopped
1 cup chocolate chips

In mixing bowl, combine brown sugar, oil, coffee, salt, soda, vanilla, eggs, flour, and nuts. Beat well. Pour into greased 9x13-inch pan and sprinkle with chocolate chips. Bake at 350 degrees for 25 to 30 minutes.

VERNA MILLER, Apple Creek, OH

Oatmeal Energy Bars

3 cups gluten-free oats
½ cup shredded coconut
½ cup chocolate chips
½ cup dried cranberries
¼ cup flaxseed

¼ cup chopped nuts
1 cup unsweetened applesauce
½ cup peanut butter
2 eggs
¼ teaspoon salt

Mix oats, coconut, chocolate chips, cranberries, flaxseed, and nuts. Stir in applesauce, peanut butter, eggs, and salt. Pour into greased 8x8-inch pan. Bake at 325 degrees for 15 to 17 minutes until golden.

JUDY ZIMMERMAN, East Earl, PA

Peanut Butter Tasty Cakes

2 cups sugar

½ cup butter or margarine

4 eggs

2 cups flour

2 teaspoons baking powder

¼ teaspoon salt

1 teaspoon vanilla

1 cup milk

1 cup peanut butter

2 to 3 cups chocolate chips

In mixing bowl, combine sugar and butter. Add eggs. Mix in flour, baking powder, and salt. Add vanilla and milk, stirring until well combined. Grease and flour 11x15-inch pan. Put batter in pan. Bake at 350 degrees for 20 to 25 minutes or until done. Do not overbake. Spread with peanut butter while still hot. Cool. Melt chocolate chips, stirring until smooth. Spread over cooled cake.

FRANIE DETWEILER, Edinboro, PA

Speedy Brownies

2 cups sugar	1¾ cups flour
½ cup cocoa powder	1 teaspoon salt
5 eggs	1 cup vegetable oil
1 teaspoon vanilla	1 cup semisweet chocolate chips

In mixing bowl, combine all but chocolate chips; beat until smooth. Pour into greased 9x13-inch pan. Sprinkle with chocolate chips. Bake at 350 degrees for 30 minutes or until toothpick inserted near center comes out clean. Cool on wire rack. Yields 3 dozen.

"These are simple and easy to make and ideal to take along to a finger-food dinner or a picnic."

Martha Petersheim, Junction City, OH

Indoor S'mores

12 ounces chocolate chips

1 tablespoon butter

⅓ cup light corn syrup

1 teaspoon vanilla

4 cups Golden Grahams cereal

1½ cups mini marshmallows

In saucepan over low heat, heat chips, butter, and corn syrup, stirring to melt. Add vanilla. Stir in cereal. Fold in marshmallows. Press into lightly greased 9x13-inch pan. When cool, cut into pieces.

Anna M. Byler, Clymer, PA

Apple Bars

1 cup flour

1 cup oats

1 cup brown sugar, divided

½ teaspoon baking soda

½ teaspoon salt

½ cup butter

2½ cups finely chopped apples

2 tablespoons butter, cut

Mix flour, oats, ½ cup brown sugar, baking soda, salt, and ½ cup butter until crumbly. Press half of mixture into 8x8-inch pan. Combine apples and ½ cup brown sugar; spread over crust. Dot with butter. Top with remaining crumb mixture. Bake at 350 degrees for 40 minutes or until golden brown. Serve warm with milk or ice cream.

Esther P. Mast, Gambier, OH

Banana Cake

½ cup shortening

1½ cups sugar

2 eggs

1 cup mashed bananas (about 3)

1 teaspoon vanilla

2 cups flour

1 teaspoon baking soda

⅓ teaspoon salt

½ cup sour milk or buttermilk

½ cup chopped walnuts

Cream shortening and sugar. Add eggs one at a time, beating well after each addition. Mix in mashed bananas and vanilla. Sift dry ingredients together and add alternately with milk. Fold in nuts. Pour into greased 9x13-inch pan and bake at 350 degrees for 45 minutes.

Mrs. Norman Miller, Clark, MO

Dark Chocolate Cake

1¾ cups flour

2 cups sugar

¾ cup cocoa powder

1½ teaspoons baking powder

1 teaspoon salt

2 eggs

1 cup milk

½ cup vegetable oil

2 teaspoons vanilla

1 cup hot water

Mix all ingredients well. Batter will be very thin. Pour into greased 9x13-inch pan and bake at 350 degrees for 35 to 40 minutes. It is a very moist cake.

Sara Hochstetler, Keytesville, MO

Bean Cake

2½ cups cooked black beans

6 eggs

¼ cup honey or ¼ teaspoon stevia

1 teaspoon vanilla

1½ teaspoons baking powder

1 teaspoon baking soda

1 teaspoon salt

¼ cup butter or other fat

½ cup shredded coconut

½ cup chopped nuts

¾ cup grated zucchini, carrot, or apple

Mash beans. Add remaining ingredients. Mix well. Pour into greased 9x9-inch pan. Bake at 350 degrees for 30 to 40 minutes until cake tests done.

Lena Troyer, Redding, IA

Dump Cake

1 cup cherry pie filling

1 can (15½ ounce) crushed pineapple, undrained

1 yellow cake mix

1 cup nuts, chopped

1 cup coconut, flaked

2 sticks margarine, melted

Spread pie filling and pineapple in ungreased 9x12-inch pan. Sprinkle dry cake mix over fruit. Top evenly with nuts and coconut. Drizzle melted margarine over all. Bake at 350 degrees for 70 minutes. Cool completely before cutting.

Mrs. Andrew J. Hostetler, Homerville, OH

Maple Pudding Cake

1 cup flour
2 teaspoons baking powder
¼ teaspoon salt
½ cup sugar
½ cup milk

2 tablespoons butter or
 softened shortening
1 cup nuts, chopped
1 cup maple syrup
¾ cup boiling water
Whipped cream

In large bowl, combine flour, baking powder, salt, and sugar. Mix in milk and butter. Stir in nuts. Spread batter in 2-quart baking dish. Combine maple syrup and boiling water. Pour over batter. Bake at 350 degrees for 40 to 45 minutes. The cake will rise to the top, and the sauce will settle to the bottom. Serve warm with whipped cream.

Susie Miller, Medford, WI

Lemon Pudding Cake

8 eggs, separated
⅔ cup lemon juice
2 teaspoons lemon zest
2 tablespoons butter, melted

3 cups sugar
1 cup flour
1 teaspoon salt
3 cups milk

Beat egg yolks, lemon juice, lemon zest, and butter. Combine sugar, flour, and salt; add to egg mixture alternately with milk. Beat egg whites until stiff and fold into batter. Pour into greased 9x13-inch pan. Set pan inside larger pan of hot water in oven. Bake at 350 degrees for 45 minutes.

Ellen Yoder, Scottville, MI

Shoofly Cake

4 cups flour	2 cups boiling water
2 cups brown sugar	1 cup molasses
¾ cup shortening	1 tablespoon baking soda

In bowl, mix flour, brown sugar, and shortening until crumbly. Set aside 1 cup. In another bowl, mix boiling water, molasses, and baking soda. Add to first mixture, stirring slightly. Pour into 9x13-inch pan. Sprinkle top with reserved crumbs. Bake at 350 degrees for 40 to 45 minutes or at 300 degrees for 1 hour.

LENA TROYER, Redding, IA
MARY ELLEN WENGERD, Campbellsville, KY

Stove-Top Custard

2 cups milk

2 eggs, beaten

½ cup sugar (or less)

1 teaspoon vanilla

Dash salt

Dash nutmeg

In mixing bowl, mix all ingredients just until blended. Pour into 4 custard cups (or coffee cups) and set cups in kettle with an inch or two of cold water (pan should have a tight-fitting lid). Bring to boil, turn off heat, and let set for 45 minutes. Unbelievable, but this makes perfect custard.

Clara Yoder, Windsor, MO

Bread Custard Pudding

2 cups bread crumbs

2½ cups milk

4 eggs

¾ cup sugar

¼ teaspoon salt

1 teaspoon vanilla

1 teaspoon nutmeg

Break up bread into 1-quart baking dish. In saucepan, scald milk. In bowl, beat eggs, sugar, salt, and vanilla. Mix well, then add milk to egg mixture. Pour over bread. Sprinkle with nutmeg. Place dish in larger pan with 1½ inches water. Bake at 350 degrees for 40 minutes.

BAKED CARAMEL APPLES

Apples
2 heaping tablespoons
    clear gelatin
1¾ cups brown sugar
Pinch salt

3 cups water
Chunk of butter
1 teaspoon vanilla
Whipped cream

Preheat oven to 350 degrees. Peel enough apples to fill 9x13-inch pan. Cut in half, core, and line pan with apple halves. In saucepan, combine gelatin, brown sugar, salt, and water. Cook until thick, stirring constantly. Add butter and vanilla. Pour over apples. Bake at 350 degrees until apples are soft. Serve with whipped cream on top.

LIZZIE MILLER (*THE SIMPLE LIFE*)

COOKED SWEET RICE

2 cups water
1 cup rice
1 teaspoon salt

2 tablespoons butter
½ cup sugar
2 cups milk

Bring water to boil and add rice, salt, and butter. Cover and simmer for 30 to 40 minutes. When water is cooked down, add sugar and milk. Bring to boil, remove from heat, and let sit until fluffy and thick.

CRYSTAL ROPP, Kalona, IA

BROWN BETTY

1 cup quick oats
1 cup flour
¾ cup brown sugar
Pinch salt

1 teaspoon baking soda
½ cup butter
2 cups sliced or shredded apples

Mix oats, flour, brown sugar, salt, and baking soda. Blend in butter. Spread half of batter in 4x9-inch pan. Top with apples. Crumble remaining batter on top. Bake at 350 degrees for 30 minutes.

VERNA STUTZMAN, Navarre, OH

Magic Cobbler

½ cup butter

¾ cup milk

2 cups sugar, divided

1 cup flour

1½ teaspoons baking powder

2 cups fruit (peaches, apples, blueberries, blackberries, etc.)

In 8x11-inch pan, melt butter. In mixing bowl, combine milk, 1 cup sugar, flour, and baking powder. Pour mixture over melted butter, but do not stir. Spread fruit on top and sprinkle with remaining 1 cup sugar. Again, do not stir. Bake at 350 degrees for 30 to 40 minutes or until fruit is soft.

ROSANNA HELMUTH, Arthur, IL

Peach Cobbler

1 cup flour

1 cup sugar

½ teaspoon salt

2 teaspoons baking powder

¾ cup milk

½ stick margarine, melted

2½ to 3 cups sliced peaches

Mix flour, sugar, salt, baking powder, and milk. Pour into baking dish and level. Pour margarine on top, but do not stir. Place peaches on top and bake at 350 degrees for 40 to 45 minutes.

RHODA M. SCHWARTZ, Decatur, IN

Shortcake Delight

4 eggs, beaten

⅓ cup sugar

½ cup oil

2 tablespoons baking powder

2 teaspoons salt

2 cups milk, divided

4 cups flour

In bowl, stir together eggs, sugar, and oil. Add baking powder, salt, and 1 cup milk, mixing well. Add flour and remaining 1 cup milk. Mix well. Pour into greased 9x13-inch pan. Bake at 350 degrees for 15 to 18 minutes or until golden brown.

"This recipe is easy enough for five-year-olds to make."

KAREN MILLER, Monroe, WI

CHEESECAKE

1 large box gelatin (your
   flavor choice)

1 cup hot water

1 sleeve graham crackers

4 tablespoons butter

1 (8 ounce) package cream
   cheese, softened

1 cup sugar

1 teaspoon vanilla

1 large can evaporated milk
   or 1½ cups cream, chilled

In bowl, dissolve gelatin in hot water; chill in refrigerator until it just starts to thicken. Meanwhile, crush graham crackers and mix in butter. Press into bottom of 9x13-inch pan, saving ⅛ cup for garnish. In bowl, combine cream cheese and sugar, then vanilla. Beat cold milk until thickened. Add to cream cheese mixture, then add combined milk mixture to gelatin. Beat until fluffy. Pour over graham cracker crust. Sprinkle remaining crumbs on top. Refrigerate until set.

"I like to take this to church suppers."

Mrs. Ervin (Susan) Byler, Crab Orchard, KY

ICE CREAM DESSERT

1 (4 quart) bucket
  vanilla ice cream
1 (4 quart) bucket
  chocolate ice cream

2 (8 ounce) tubs
  whipped topping
1 package Oreo
  cookies, crushed

Soften ice cream for 15 minutes. In bowl, use electric mixer to mix vanilla ice cream with 8 ounces whipped topping. In separate bowl, mix chocolate ice cream with remaining 8 ounces whipped topping. Layer both mixtures into two 9x13-inch pans as follows: chocolate ice cream, half of cookie crumbs, vanilla ice cream, remaining cookie crumbs. Freeze. May also be prepared in individual cups.

ANNA M. BYLER, Clymer, PA

IMPOSSIBLE-TO-RUIN PIE

2 cups milk
4 eggs, beaten
½ teaspoon salt
1 tablespoon vanilla

½ cup flour
½ cup sweetener (sugar,
   honey, maple syrup)
1 cup coconut

Blend everything together. Pour into glass pie pan. Bake at 350 degrees for 45 minutes just until set. No piecrust needed!

RACHEL YODER, Fultonville, NY

WANDA'S NO-SUGAR APPLE PIE

8 cups sliced Yellow
   Delicious apples
1 can frozen apple
   juice concentrate
2 tablespoons butter

1 teaspoon cinnamon
½ teaspoon nutmeg
4 tablespoons instant tapioca
1 baked pie shell

In saucepan, cook apples in apple juice. Add butter, cinnamon, nutmeg, and tapioca. When apples are tender, pour into baked pie shell.

WANDA E. BRUNSTETTER

SIMPLE SNACKS

*Enjoy the little things, for one day you may look
back and discover they were the big things.*

UNKNOWN

Daily Green Bomb

1½ cups frozen mango chunks
2 celery stalks, chunked
1 large cucumber, thickly sliced
1 banana, chunked and frozen
½ cup parsley
½ cup cilantro

3 cups coconut water
1 tablespoon lemon juice
1 tablespoon lime juice
Water
Ice

Blend all ingredients except water and ice in heavy-duty blender. Add water and ice to reach desired consistency. Blend more if needed. Divide into 4 glasses or 4 pint jars, close tightly, and store in refrigerator. Use within 3 days.

KATHRYN TROYER, Rutherford, TN

Effortless Eggnog

½ gallon cold milk, divided
1 (3.4 ounce) package French
    vanilla instant pudding mix
¼ cup sugar

2 teaspoons vanilla
½ teaspoon cinnamon
½ teaspoon nutmeg

In large bowl, whisk ¾ cup milk and pudding mix until smooth. Whisk in sugar, vanilla, cinnamon, and nutmeg. Stir in remaining milk. Refrigerate until serving. Yields 2 quarts.

ROSELLA OBERHOLTZER, Mifflinburg, PA

Strawberry Mizz Fizz

½ cup strawberries
¼ cup milk
¾ cup sugar
½ teaspoon vanilla

¼ cup strawberry or vanilla ice cream
¼ cup club soda

Blend strawberries, milk, sugar, vanilla, and ice cream in blender. Then add soda in on-and-off pulsing motion until combined. Pour into chilled glass.

Mary K. Bontrager, Middlebury, IN

Simple Smoothie

1 banana
2 cups frozen strawberries
¾ cup frozen blueberries

1 cup unsweetened apple juice
2 scoops unflavored collagen powder

Layer in blender in order: banana, strawberries, blueberries, apple juice, and collagen. Blend until smooth. Yields 4 cups.

Mary Miller, Shipshewana, IN

Cucumber Spread

1 cucumber, chopped

1 small onion, chopped

1 (8 ounce) package cream cheese, softened

Place cucumber and onion in blender or food processor; puree. Drain most of the juice from vegetables through strainer, then blend vegetables into cream cheese. Refrigerate for at least 12 hours before serving on crackers or party rye bread.

Cheddar Bacon Dip

1 (8 ounce) package cream cheese, softened

1 package dry ranch dressing mix

1 (3 ounce) bag real bacon bits

2 cups shredded cheddar cheese

1 (16 ounce) container sour cream

In bowl, combine all ingredients. Mix well. Transfer to 2-quart baking dish, cover, and bake at 350 degrees for 25 to 30 minutes or until hot and bubbly.

Ann M. Miller, Decatur, IN

Buffalo Chicken Dip

2 cups cooked chicken

2 cups shredded cheese

1 (8 ounce) package
cream cheese

1 cup ranch dressing

½ cup buffalo sauce

Mix all together and bake at 350 degrees for 30 minutes.

Amanda Rose Esh, Parkesburg, PA

Cheesy Hamburger Dip

1 box Velveeta cheese
1 pound ground beef

1 envelope taco seasoning
16 ounces salsa

In glass dish in 350-degree oven (or use slow cooker), melt cheese, stirring often until smooth. Meanwhile, in skillet, fry ground beef and drain grease. Add taco seasoning. Mix beef and salsa into melted cheese. Bake at 350 degrees for 12 to 15 minutes until hot. Serve with chips or crackers.

Mary K. Bontrager, Middlebury, IN

Hot Pizza Dip

1 (8 ounce) package
   cream cheese
1 (8 ounce) carton sour cream
1 teaspoon oregano

⅛ teaspoon garlic powder
Pinch red pepper
1 cup pizza sauce
½ cup chopped pepperoni

In bowl, mix cream cheese, sour cream, oregano, garlic powder, and red pepper. Pour in 9x9-inch pan. Spread with pizza sauce. Top with pepperoni. Bake uncovered at 350 degrees for 20 minutes. Serve with bread, chips, etc.

Moses Riehl, Coatesville, PA

Chili-Corn Dip

1 (15 ounce) can corn, drained

1 (4 ounce) can chopped green chilies, undrained

1 cup sour cream

½ cup ranch dressing

4 teaspoons dry ranch dressing or dip powder

1 teaspoon pepper

½ teaspoon garlic powder

¾ cup fried and crumbled bacon pieces, plus more if desired

1 cup shredded cheddar cheese, plus more if desired

Scoop-style corn chips or club crackers

In mixing bowl, combine corn, chilies, sour cream, dressing, dry ranch powder, pepper, and garlic powder; add bacon and cheese. Additional cheese and bacon pieces may be added. Refrigerate. Serve with corn chips or crackers.

Mary Miller, Shipshewana, IN

Black Bean Dip

1 (15 ounce) can black beans,
  drained and rinsed
1 cup frozen corn kernels
1 small green pepper, chopped
2 Roma tomatoes, chopped
1 tablespoon lemon juice
2 teaspoons chopped cilantro

½ teaspoon salt
Pepper to taste
Chili powder to taste
Hot sauce to taste
¼ cup Italian dressing
Scoop-style tortilla chips

In bowl, mix together beans, corn, green pepper, tomatoes, lemon juice, cilantro, salt, pepper, chili powder, hot sauce, and dressing. Chill. Serve with tortilla chip scoops.

Lela Brenneman, Danville, AL

Cauliflower Bean Dip

1 head cauliflower

1 can cannellini (white kidney) beans, drained and rinsed

3 cloves garlic

1 teaspoon salt

1 teaspoon thyme

2 teaspoons cumin

⅓ cup lemon juice

¼ cup olive oil

Roast cauliflower (covered) in oven at 350 degrees for 1 hour. Blend cauliflower with remaining ingredients in blender or food processor. Serve with corn chips or crackers.

Anna M. Byler, Belleville, PA

Loaded Baked Potato Dip

2 cups sour cream

2 cups shredded cheddar cheese

8 slices bacon, fried and crumbled

2 teaspoons hot sauce

Mix all together and serve with waffle fries or potato chips.

Mary Ann Byler, New Wilmington, PA

REFRIGERATOR PICKLES

6 cups thinly sliced cucumbers

2 cups sugar

1 cup white vinegar

1 tablespoon salt

1 teaspoon celery seed (optional)

1 cup sliced green pepper

1 cup sliced onion

Mix all ingredients together, cover, and refrigerate. Ready to eat in 24 hours. These will keep for a long time. Can also be frozen.

ROSE MARIE SHETLER, Berne, IN

MARY ANN YUTZY, Bloomfield, IA

Popcorn Snack

½ cup margarine or butter

½ cup vegetable oil

1 (16 ounce) bag mini
marshmallows

1 teaspoon vanilla

½ teaspoon salt

6 quarts popped popcorn

1 pound chocolate candies

1 pound dry-roasted peanuts

In saucepan, melt margarine, oil, and marshmallows over low heat. Add vanilla and salt. In bowl, combine popcorn, candies, and peanuts. Pour buttery sauce over all and mix well. Spread out to cool and dry. Store in airtight containers.

Mrs. Albert Yoder, Stanwood, MI

Cashew Crunch

1 pound butter
1 pound sugar

1 pound raw cashews

Cook butter and sugar together over high heat to 248 degrees. Then add cashews and stir until cashews are golden brown. Pour into large greased pan. Let cool, then break into pieces.

Verna Stutzman, Navarre, OH

Ranch Party Mix

1 cup oil
1 package ranch dip mix
1 round tablespoon sour
   cream and onion powder

2 pounds snack mix of
choice, such as a mix of
pretzels, Bugles, crackers,
peanuts, Corn Chex,
Kix, Honeycomb, etc.

Mix together first 3 ingredients. Add snack mix. Mix well, then bake at 250 degrees for 1 hour in cake pan; stirring every 15 minutes.

Doris Schlabach, Goshen, IN

Sweet and Salty Snack Mix

1 (11 ounce) bag pretzels
1 (10 ounce) package mini
   cheese-filled crackers
1 cup dry-roasted peanuts
1 cup sugar
½ cup butter

½ cup light corn syrup
2 tablespoons vanilla
1 teaspoon baking soda
1 (10 ounce) bag M&M's
1 (18½ ounce) package
   candy corn

In large bowl, combine pretzels, crackers, and peanuts. In large saucepan, combine sugar, butter, and corn syrup. Bring to boil over medium heat; boil for 5 minutes. Remove from heat; stir in vanilla and baking soda (mixture will foam). Pour over pretzel mixture and stir until coated. Pour into greased 10x15x1-inch baking pan. Bake at 250 degrees for 45 minutes, stirring every 10 to 15 minutes. Break apart while warm. Toss with M&M's and candy corn. Cool completely. Store mix in airtight containers. Yields 16 cups.

Doretta Yoder, Topeka, IN

QUICK BREADS

But he giveth more grace. Wherefore he saith, God resisteth the proud, but giveth grace unto the humble.

JAMES 4:6

Pumpkin Bran Muffins

4 eggs

2 cups sugar

1½ cups vegetable oil

2 teaspoons baking powder

2 teaspoons baking soda

1 teaspoon salt

1 teaspoon cinnamon

2 cups mashed cooked pumpkin

3 cups bran

2 cups flour

1 cup raisins

In large bowl, beat eggs; add sugar, oil, baking powder, baking soda, salt, cinnamon, and pumpkin. Beat well. Add bran, flour, and raisins. Stir until well blended. Spoon into greased muffin tins and bake at 350 degrees for 20 minutes. Yields 2½ dozen.

LENA MARTIN, Trenton, KY

Best Ever Banana Bread

1¾ cups flour
1 teaspoon baking soda
1½ cups sugar
½ teaspoon salt
2 eggs
2 medium ripe bananas, mashed

½ cup vegetable oil
¼ cup plus 1 tablespoon buttermilk
1 teaspoon vanilla
1 cup chopped walnuts

In large bowl, sift together flour, baking soda, sugar, and salt. In another bowl, combine eggs, bananas, oil, buttermilk, and vanilla. Add mixture to flour mixture, stirring until just combined. Fold in nuts. Bake in greased and floured loaf pan. Bake at 350 degrees for 1 hour. Cool on wire rack.

Mary Ellen Wengerd, Campbellsville, KY

Harvest Loaf

1¾ cups flour
1 teaspoon baking soda
1 teaspoon cinnamon
½ teaspoon nutmeg
¼ teaspoon ginger
¼ teaspoon ground cloves

½ cup butter
1 cup sugar
2 eggs
¾ cup pumpkin puree
½ cup chocolate chips
¼ cup raisins or nuts

Mix all ingredients together. Bake in greased loaf pan at 350 degrees for 60 minutes.

Mary Jane Kuepfer, Chesley, Ontario, Canada

Pumpkin Bread

4 eggs

3 cups sugar

1 teaspoon cinnamon

⅔ cup water

1 cup olive oil

1 cup chopped nuts

½ teaspoon salt

1 teaspoon nutmeg

2 cups pumpkin puree

2 teaspoons baking soda

3½ cups flour

In large bowl, beat eggs; add remaining ingredients and mix well. Pour into 3 well-greased loaf pans. Bake at 300 degrees for 1 hour or until done in center. This bread freezes well.

Katie Yoder, Fultonville, NY

Zucchini Bread

4 cups flour

1 teaspoon baking soda

1 teaspoon salt

½ teaspoon baking powder

2 teaspoons cinnamon

½ teaspoon nutmeg

¼ teaspoon cloves

3 eggs, beaten

1 cup oil

2 cups brown sugar

3 teaspoons vanilla

3 cups shredded zucchini

1 cup chopped nuts

Mix all ingredients well and put in 3 or 4 greased bread pans. Bake at 350 degrees for 1 hour. Serve plain or frosted with caramel icing.

Martha Beechy, Butler, OH

HEALTH BREAD

2 cups bran flakes or
all-bran cereal

2 cups buttermilk

4 teaspoons molasses

1 cup raisins

2 teaspoons baking soda

2 cups flour

¼ cup sweetener of choice

Combine all ingredients in large bowl. Pour into large, greased loaf pan or 2 small loaf pans. Bake at 350 degrees for 45 to 60 minutes.

DAVID C. P. SCHWARTZ, Galesburg, KS

PEPPERONI BREAD

1 pound (or 1 recipe)
pizza dough

5 tablespoons butter, melted

¼ teaspoon garlic powder

½ teaspoon parsley

¼ teaspoon seasoned salt

1 to 2 cups pepperoni

2 cups mozzarella cheese

Roll dough out to 10x15-inch rectangle. In small bowl, mix together butter, garlic powder, parsley, and seasoned salt. Spread about 3 tablespoons butter over dough. Layer pepperoni on dough. Top with cheese. Start from short end and roll up dough like a jelly roll. Fold ends under and seal. Place seam-side down on greased baking sheet. Brush top with remaining butter. Bake at 350 degrees for 30 minutes. Slice and enjoy while warm.

NORMA YUTZY, Drakesville, IA

Cheddar Spoon Bread

2 cups milk, divided

½ cup cornmeal

1 cup shredded cheddar cheese

⅓ cup butter

1 tablespoon sugar

1 teaspoon salt

2 eggs, well beaten

In saucepan, scald 1½ cups milk (heat to 180 degrees). In mixing bowl, mix cornmeal with remaining ½ cup cold milk and add to hot milk. Cook, stirring constantly, over low heat until thickened, approximately 5 minutes. Add cheese, butter, sugar, and salt; stir until melted. Remove from heat; stir in eggs. Pour into 1-quart greased baking dish. Bake at 350 degrees for about 35 minutes or until lightly browned and set. Serve immediately. Yields 6 servings.

LAURA MILLER, Fredericktown, OH

No-Knead Whole Wheat Bread

1 tablespoon yeast
1¼ cups warm water
2 tablespoons butter, melted
1 teaspoon salt

1½ cups whole wheat flour
1½ cups all-purpose flour
1 egg

Mix all ingredients and set aside to rise until doubled in size—about 30 minutes. Stir dough 30 strokes with spoon. Pour batter into greased loaf pan. Cover and let rise in warm place. Bake at 350 degrees for 30 minutes.

Anna Yoder, Fairchild, WI

Index of Contributors

INDEX OF RECIPES BY SECTION

Index of Recipes by Key Ingredients

One-Pan Breakfasts

O satisfy us early with thy mercy; that we may rejoice and be glad all our days.

Psalm 90:14

FARMER'S BREAKFAST

½ pound bacon

1 onion, chopped

3 cooked potatoes,
    cubed or shredded

5 eggs

Salt and pepper to taste

1 cup shredded cheddar cheese

Chopped fresh parsley

In skillet, cook bacon and onions until bacon is crisp. Remove bacon and onions from skillet. Drain all but ½ cup drippings. Add potatoes and brown. Return bacon and onions to skillet. Make 5 wells in potatoes and break 1 egg into each. Season with salt and pepper; sprinkle with cheese. Cover and cook on low heat for 5 to 10 minutes or until eggs are set. Garnish with parsley. Serve immediately.

KATIE ZOOK, Apple Creek, OH